Biogra

James Egan was born in 1985 and
Co. Laois in the Midlands of Irela
In 2008, James moved to England
James married his wife in 2012 and currently lives in Havant in Hampshire.
James had his first book, 365 Ways to Stop Sabotaging Your Life, published in 2014.
Several of James' books have become No.1 Best Sellers in the UK including 1000 Facts about Horror Movies, 3000 Facts About the Greatest Movies Ever, 365 Things People Believe That Aren't True, Another 365 Things People Believe That Aren't True, and 500 Things People Believe That Aren't True.

Books by James Egan
Fairytale
Inherit the Earth
Inherit the Earth: The Animal Kingdom
1000 Facts About the United States
Words That Need to Exist in English
Hilarious Things That Kids Say
Hilarious Things That Mums Say
1000 Facts about TV Shows Vol. 1-3
1000 Facts about Animated Shows Vol. 1-3
1000 Facts about Actors Vol. 1-3
1000 Facts about Countries Vol. 1-3
Dinosaurs Had Feathers (and other Random Facts)
1000 Facts about Animals Vol. 1-3
1000 Facts about James Bond
1000 Inspiring Facts
How to Psychologically Survive Cancer
1000 Out-of-this-World Facts about Space
1000 Facts about the Greatest Movies Ever Vol. 1-3
1000 Facts about Film Directors
1000 Facts about Superhero Movies Vol. 1-3
1000 Facts about Superheroes Vol. 1-3
1000 Facts about Supervillains Vol. 1-3
1000 Facts about Comic Books Vol. 1-3
1000 Facts about Animated Films Vol. 1-3
1000 Facts about Horror Movies Vol. 1-3
1000 Facts about American Presidents
Adorable Animal Facts
1000 Facts about Video Games Vol. 1-3
Things People Believe That Aren't True Vol. 1-4
1000 Fact about Film Director
The Mega Misconception Book
3000 Astounding Quotes
1000 Facts About Comic Book Characters Vol. 1-3
100 Classic Stories in 100 Pages
500 Facts about Godzilla
365 Ways to Stop Sabotaging Your Life
Flat Earthers Around the Globe
1000 Facts about Historic Figures Vol. 1-3
1000 Facts About Writers
1000 Facts about Ireland
The Biggest Movie Plotholes
1000 Facts about the Human Body

100 Classic Stories in 100 Pages

By

James Egan

Copyright 2015 © James Egan

All rights reserved. No part of this book may be reproduced, stored, or transmitted by any means - whether auditory, graphic, mechanical, or electronic - without written permission of both publisher and author, except in the case of brief excerpts used in critical articles and reviews. Unauthorized reproduction of any part of this work is illegal and is punishable by law.

ISBN: 9781326235642

Because of the dynamic nature of the Internet, any web addresses or links contained in this book may have changed since publication and may no longer be valid. The views expressed in this work are solely those of the author and do not necessarily reflect the views of the publisher, and the publisher hereby disclaims any responsibility for them.

Any people depicted in stock imagery provided by Thinkstock are models, and such images are being used for illustrative purposes only.

Lulu Publishing Services rev. date: 31/05/2015

For Shannon
A wonderful human being who has irrevocably
influenced my life for the better

Introduction

According to a survey of 2,000 people in the UK, 65% of them have pretended to read classic novels.

Nineteen-Eighty Four was ranked #1 as the most common book that people pretend to have read. 42% in the survey pretended they have read this classic story.

Second on the poll is Leo Tolstoy's masterpiece, War and Peace (31%), third is James Joyce's novel, Ulysses (25%) and fourth was the Bible (24%.)

In a way, it's easy to pretend people have read classic novels because there are so many film adaptations. The majority of society can say they know stories like Frankenstein or Dracula.

Even if you haven't read classics like The Adventures of Huckleberry Finn, Doctor Faustus, or Oliver Twist, it's easy to create a mental image that encapsulates these stories.

A kid on a raft in overalls wearing a straw hat.

A man selling his soul to the devil.

An orphan begging for gruel.

You might have an understanding of the outline of a lot of stories that you haven't read. But do you know the ins-and-outs of these wondrous tales?

Are you basing your knowledge entirely on a film adaptation?

Did you know that the Frankenstein and Dracula films are drastically different from the book?

Have your friends ever talked about Little Women or Great Expectations and you didn't have a clue what they were talking about?

Were you ever curious to know what the big deal is about this Long John Silver character you keep hearing about or who the heck is Captain Nemo and what the devil is Hamlet talking about in that "To be or not to be" speech?

You were always curious about these stories. You have been hearing about them for years, perhaps decades.

But you haven't read them.

But you may feel like it's not your fault. Maybe you want to read classics like Treasure Island or 20,000 Leagues Under the Sea but you just never seemed to have time.

It's a fair excuse. Books can be a huge commitment. War and Peace is 1,225 pages long. Hamlet takes four-and-a-half hours to perform fully and is mostly written in iambic pentameter. That language is confusing to someone unfamiliar with Shakespeare. It's difficult to someone who IS familiar with Shakespeare!

That's why I have summarized all of these stories in one page each. You shouldn't use this as an excuse to avoid reading any of these classic stories (although it will save you reading about 50,000 pages.) If you find these summaries interesting, check out the actual books.

Contents

1.	**The Epic of Gilgamesh** by Anon – 1800 BC	p11
2.	**The Iliad** by Homer – 750 BC	p12
3.	**The Odyssey** by Homer – 740 BC	p13
4.	**Antigone** by Sophocles – 441 BC	p14
5.	**Medea** by Euripides – 431 BC	p15
6.	**Oedipus the King** by Sophocles – 429 BC	p16
7.	**Electra** by Sophocles – 404 BC	p17
8.	**The Brothers Menaechmus** by Plautus – Approx. 170 BC	p18
9.	**The Aeneid** by Virgil – 19 BC	p19
10.	**Beowulf** by Anon – 1025	p20
11.	**1001 Arabian Nights** by Various Authors – 1300	p21
12.	**Doctor Faustus** by Christopher Marlowe – 1592	p22
13.	**A Midsummer Night's Dream** by William Shakespeare – 1596	p23
14.	**Romeo and Juliet** by William Shakespeare – 1597	p24
15.	**Hamlet** by William Shakespeare – 1599	p25
16.	**Julius Caesar** by William Shakespeare – 1599	p26
17.	**King Lear** by William Shakespeare – 1603	p27
18.	**Othello** by William Shakespeare – 1603	p28
19.	**Don Quixote** by Miguel de Cervantes Savedra – 1605	p29
20.	**Macbeth** by William Shakespeare – 1606	p30
21.	**Paradise Lost** by John Milton – 1667	p31
22.	**Robinson Crusoe** by Daniel Defoe – 1719	p32
23.	**Gulliver's Travels** by Jonathan Swift – 1726	p33
24.	**Tom Jones** by Henry Fielding – 1749	p34
25.	**Sense and Sensibility** by Jane Austen – 1811	p35
26.	**Pride and Prejudice** by Jane Austen – 1813	p36
27.	**Emma** by Jane Austen – 1815	p37
28.	**Frankenstein** by Mary Shelley – 1818	p38
29.	**Oliver Twist** by Charles Dickens – 1838	p39
30.	**Nicholas Nickleby** by Charles Dickens – 1839	p40
31.	**The Pit and the Pendulum** by Edgar Allen Poe – 1842	p41
32.	**The Tell-Tale Heart** by Edgar Allen Poe – 1843	p42
33.	**The Three Musketeers** by Alexandre Dumas – 1844	p43
34.	**The Count of Monte Cristo** by Alexandre Dumas – 1844	p44
35.	**The Snow Queen** by Hans Christian Anderson – 1844	p45
36.	**Wuthering Heights** by Emily Bronte – 1847	p46
37.	**Jane Eyre** by Charlotte Bronte – 1847	p47
38.	**David Copperfield** by Charles Dickens – 1849	p48
39.	**The Scarlet Letter** by Nathaniel Hawthorne – 1850	p49
40.	**Moby Dick** by Herman Melville – 1851	p50
41.	**A Tale of Two Cities** by Charles Dickens – 1859	p51
42.	**Great Expectations** by Charles Dickens – 1861	p52
43.	**Journey to the Centre of the Earth** by Jules Verne – 1864	p53
44.	**Our Mutual Friend** by Charles Dickens – 1865	p54
45.	**Crime and Punishment** by Fyodor Dostoevsky – 1866	p55
46.	**Little Women** by Louisa May Alcott – 1868	p56

47.	**War and Peace** by Leo Tolstoy – 1869	p57
48.	**The Idiot** by Fyodor Dostoevsky – 1869	p58
49.	**20,000 Leagues Under the Sea** by Jules Verne – 1870	p59
50.	**Around the World in Eighty Days** by Jules Verne – 1873	p60
51.	**The Mysterious Island** by Jules Verne – 1874	p61
52.	**The Adventures of Tom Sawyer** by Mark Twain – 1876	p62
53.	**Anna Karenina** by Leo Tolstoy – 1877	p63
54.	**Treasure Island** by Robert Louis Stevenson – 1883	p64
55.	**The Adventures of Huckleberry Finn** by Mark Twain –1884	p65
56.	**Dr. Jekyll and Mr. Hyde** by Robert Louis Stevenson – 1886	p66
57.	**The Picture of Dorian Gray** by Oscar Wilde – 1891	p67
58.	**The Time Machine** by HG Wells – 1895	p68
59.	**The Importance of Being Earnest** by Oscar Wilde – 1895	p69
60.	**The Island of Doctor Moreau** by HG Wells – 1896	p70
61.	**The Seagull** by Anton Chekhov – 1896	p71
62.	**Dracula** by Bram Stoker – 1897	p72
63.	**The Invisible Man** by HG Wells – 1897	p73
64.	**Heart of Darkness** by Joseph Conrad – 1899	p74
65.	**The Three Sisters** by Anton Chekhov – 1901	p75
66.	**Nostromo** by Joseph Conrad – 1904	p76
67.	**The Wind in the Willows** by Kenneth Grahame – 1908	p77
68.	**Howard's End** by E.M. Forster – 1910	p78
69.	**The Metamorphosis** by Franz Kafka – 1915	p79
70.	**A Portrait of the Artist as a Young Man** by James Joyce – 1916	p80
71.	**The Great Gatsby** by F. Scott Fitzgerald – 1925	p81
72.	**The Maltese Falcon** by Dashiell Hammett – 1929	p82
73.	**Brave New World** by Aldous Huxley – 1932	p83
74.	**Of Mice and Men** by John Steinbeck – 1937	p84
75.	**Rebecca** by Daphne de Maurier – 1938	p85
76.	**The Grapes of Wrath** by John Steinbeck – 1939	p86
77.	**The Big Sleep** by Raymond Chandler – 1939	p87
78.	**Animal Farm** by George Orwell – 1945	p88
79.	**All My Sons** by Arthur Miller – 1947	p89
80.	**The Pearl** by John Steinbeck – 1947	p90
81.	**Nineteen-Eighty Four** by George Orwell – 1949	p91
82.	**Death of a Salesman** by Arthur Miller – 1949	p92
83.	**The Old Man and the Sea** by Ernest Hemingway – 1951	p93
84.	**Catcher in the Rye** by J.D. Salinger – 1951	p94
85.	**East of Eden** by John Steinbeck – 1952	p95
86.	**The Crucible** by Arthur Miller – 1953	p96
87.	**Fahrenheit 451** by Ray Bradbury – 1953	p97
88.	**Waiting for Godot** by Samuel Beckett – 1953	p98
89.	**Lord of the Flies** by William Golding – 1954	p99
90.	**Atlas Shrugged** by Ayn Rand – 1957	p100
91.	**Things Fall Apart** by Chinua Achebe – 1958	p101
92.	**To Kill a Mockingbird** by Harper Lee – 1960	p102
93.	**Catch-22** by Joseph Heller – 1961	p103
94.	**Dune** by Frank Herbert – 1965	p104
95.	**Slaughterhouse Five** by Kurt Vonnegut – 1969	p105
96.	**Watership Down** by Richard Adams – 1972	p106
97.	**The Stand** by Stephen King – 1978	p107

98.	**Beloved** by Toni Morrison – 1987	p108
99.	**The Remains of the Day** by Kazuo Ishiguro – 1989	p109
100.	**The Kite Runner** by Khaled Hosseini – 2003	p110

1.
The Epic of Gilgamesh
By Anon
1800 BC

A demi-god begins a journey to become immortal.

The demi-god, King Gilgamesh, builds the great city of Uruk in Mesopotamia. He oppresses his people with intense work and forces himself on women. The people beg the gods to help them. The gods send Enkidu the wild man to kill Uruk's animals. Gilgamesh retaliates by sending a woman called Shamhat into the wild to tame Enkidu. The plan is a success.

When the pair returns to Uruk, they witness Gilgamesh demanding to sleep with a bride on her wedding day. Enkidu blocks Gilgamesh from entering the bride's wedding chamber. They fight into the night and Gilgamesh emerges victorious but he respects Enkidu for standing up to him and putting up a good fight. Gilgamesh becomes friends with Enkidu.

They decide to go on an adventure. They cross the desert and enter the Cedar forest and destroy the ogre-god, Humbaba. As they return home, Enkidu falls ill. It seems Humbaba has cursed him.

As Enkidu's health worsens, he tells Gilgamesh that he has seen the afterlife and it is terrifying. It is a place called the Netherworld. It is without light and the inhabitants are feathered and are forced to drink dirt and eat stone. The door and lock of the Netherworld is coated in thick dust because it has never been opened. But the scariest image for Gilgamesh is how the Netherworld is littered with the crowns of kings. Enkidu dies 12 days later.

Terrified that he will suffer the same fate, Gilgamesh seeks out a quest for immortality. Only two people have ever been granted immortality by the gods, Utnapishtim and his wife.

Gilgamesh journeys to the Mashu mountain which is guarded by giant scorpions. He pleads his case and the scorpions let him pass. He passes through the mountain and arrives at The Waters of Death. On The Waters, he sees a boat that will bring him to Utnapishtim. However, the Waters are guarded by stone giants. Gilgamesh quickly slays them.

A ferryman called Urshanabi appears and scolds Gilgamesh, saying that the stone-giants were the only things that could walk through The Waters and live. The only way he can get through is by cutting down the trees and building hundreds of oars for the boat.

As he crosses The Waters, the oars dissolve one by one. Urshanabi tells Gilgamesh the story of how Utnapishtim gained his eternal life. Years ago, the gods were angry at the evil of humanity and so, they flooded the world. The sky god, Ea warned Utnapishtim to build an ark that could house the seed of every creature on earth. The gods regretted what they did and promised never to attempt to destroy humanity again. As a failsafe to ensure humanity would always survive, they granted Utnapishtim and his wife immortality.

Gilgamesh arrives at Utnapishtim's island. Sadly, Utnapishtim cannot pass this power onto Gilgamesh but he tells him of a flower on the ocean floor that will make him immortal.

Gilgamesh travels to the ocean and attaches rocks to his legs so he plummets to the bottom. He finds the plant hours later and emerges out of the water triumphant. Before he has a chance to use it, a passing serpent eats the plant. The serpent sheds its skin to reveal a younger form before it slithers away.

When Gilgamesh returns to Uruk, he falls to his knees after seeing the city that he constructed. He realizes that humanity was not supposed to live forever but to accomplish great deeds that will outlive them. He has achieved this when he formed Uruk, the mightiest city in all the land.

2.
The Iliad
by Homer
750 BC

The Trojans declare a ten-year war on the Greeks.

The Trojan War began when Helen of Troy either fled or was abducted by a man called Paris. Helen's husband, Menelaus was enraged and declared war on the Greeks.

The story begins at the end of the Trojan War that has been raging on for a decade. The Greeks are laying siege to the Trojans. A Trojan priest called Chryses offers the Greek leader, Agamemnon money if they return his daughter, Chryseis but he is turned down.

Chryses prays to the god of plague, Apollo for help. Apollo sends a plague upon the Greeks, decimating their numbers. Agamemnon frees Chryseis and the plague ends.

Because of Agamemnon's poor leadership skills, the commander of the Greek army, Achilles refuses to fight. He and his men, the Myrmidons return home. Achilles asks his mother, Thetis to pray to Zeus to show that Agamemnon needs him to win the war.

Zeus makes Agamemnon dream of his army attacking the Trojans. Agamemnon awakens and checks if his remaining army still support him. He asks them to go home assuming they will stay out of loyalty. This reverse psychology backfires and they prepare to leave until a soldier called Odysseus encourages the men to stay.

Agamemnon's army makes their way to the Trojan territory. The Trojan king, Priam realizes that the Greeks are coming and he readies his soldiers.

Before they engage in an all-out war, Paris decides to have a one-on-one battle with Helen's husband, Menelaus. Menelaus effortlessly beats Paris in combat but the goddess of love, Aphrodite rescues him before Menelaus can kill him.

Paris' brother, Hector leads the Trojans and they dominate the Greeks. The gods try to influence the battle without getting directly involved. Eventually, Zeus bars the gods from any interference whatsoever.

Agamemnon realizes he will lose and sends men to Achilles who is staying at a nearby camp. The men beg him to return but he says no.

The next day Achilles sends his friend, Patroclus to learn of the war's casualties. Patroclus sees the devastation of the Greeks and rallies Achilles to enter the battle. Achilles protests but allows Patroclus to borrow Achilles' armor and his men but warns him not to directly attack the Trojans. Patroclus doesn't listen and is killed by Hector.

Achilles vows revenge against Hector. His mother is afraid because there is a prophecy that if Achilles kills Hector, he will die shortly after.

Hector has stolen Achilles' armor and so the god of metal, Hephaestus gives him new armor and a shield. Achilles drives his chariot into battle in spite of his horse, Xanthos warning Achilles that he will die if he fights.

Zeus goes back on his word and allows the gods to interfere in the war.

Achilles kills many people and eventually slays Hector. He attaches Hector's body to his chariot and drags his corpse around as punishment for killing Patroclus.

Hector's father, King Priam infiltrates the Greek camp and implores Achilles to give his son back so he can bury him. Achilles is moved to tears and agrees. Priam retrieves Hector and buries him.

3.
The Odyssey
by Homer
740 BC

Odysseus journeys for ten years to return to his family.

Odysseus' son, Telemachus, and wife, Penelope are in their home in Ithaca, waiting for Odysseus' return. A hundred men urge Penelope to let them marry her but she rejects them.

Telemachus heads to Sparta and meets Menelaus and Helen, who have reconciled their differences since the Trojan War. Menelaus tells Telemachus that on his travels, the god of rivers, Proteus said that Odysseus has been captured by the sea nymph, Calypso.

When Odysseus left Troy, his ships were caught in a storm and they landed on an island where Polyphemus the Cyclops captured him and his men. Odysseus told the Cyclops that his name was Noman. Eventually Odysseus blinded Polyphemus. The other Cyclopses heard Polyphemus screaming and asked him who was hurting him. Polyphemus shouted, "No man is hurting me!" so the Cyclopses left him in agony. As Odysseus escapes, he taunts Polyphemus by telling him his real name. Polyphemus screams for help from his father, Poseidon, the god of the sea and brother of Zeus.

After Odysseus escapes from Polyphemus, he receives a bag from the master of the winds, Aelous. This bag contains all of the wind in the world except the west wind, which is the one wind Odysseus needs to get home. As their ship is approaching Odysseus' home, the crew opens the bag while Odysseus sleeps, assuming there is gold within. As they open the bag, all of the winds burst out sending the ship far away from home.

All of Odysseus' ships are destroyed except his own. He sails until he finds the goddess of magic, Circe who tells Odysseus to make his way to the underworld.

He sails to the western edge of the world where the spirits of the dead speak to Odysseus, including his fallen comrades and Agamemnon. He sees the spirit of his mother, who tells Odysseus about the men trying to seduce his wife.

Odysseus sails on and encounters the Sirens; sea witches whose songs lure men to sail their ships into rocks. The crew plug their ears up so they can't hear the Sirens but Odysseus is curious about their music. He ties himself to the mast while his men steer the ship.

After the encounter with the Sirens, Odysseus confronts a six-headed female octopus called Scylla and a whirlpool called Charybdis.

Odysseus swims to the island of Ogygia where the beautiful sea nymph, Calypso imprisons him. Seven years later, the gods' messenger, Hermes tracks down Odysseus and demands his release. Odysseus builds a raft and leaves.

When Poseidon discovers Odysseus has escaped, the ocean god destroys his raft. Odysseus swims to Scherie, where the Phaeacians live. A girl called Nausicaa greets Odysseus and brings him to her family. He eats at the Phaeacians home, but when a musician sings about the Trojan War, Odysseus becomes overwhelmed by emotion. He tells everybody how the Trojans defeated the Greeks.

Odysseus also informs the Phaeacians about his struggle getting home. The Phaeacians agree to help Odysseus and they bring him all the way to Ithaca. He meets his son and they embrace each other. Odysseus kills all of the men who were trying to seduce his wife. He reveals himself to Penelope and the two kiss. The families of the men Odysseus killed intend to come to his home to claim revenge. The goddess of wisdom, Athena steps in and stops them saying that too much blood has already been spilt and it must end. This finally concludes the circle of violence.

4.
<u>Antigone</u>
by Sophocles
441 BC

A king experiences the wrath of the gods after he refuses to have a traitor buried.

Polyneices and Eteocles are two brothers on opposing sides of the Thebes' Civil War. They are the sons of a dead king and they fight each other, believing the victor will become the new ruler of Thebes. However, they end up killing each other and the throne goes to Creon.

The Theban people loved Eteocles so King Creon gives him an honorable burial.

However, Polynieces defected to the enemies of Thebes and so, he is seen as a traitor. As a result, Creon decides to leave his body unburied, allowing it to be eaten by vultures and worms. This is meant to be the worst punishment possible. Not even the gods tolerate this lack of respect for the dead.

Polyneices and Eteocles had sisters called Antigone and Ismene. Antigone is upset with Creon's disrespect to her brother. In spite of her brother's crimes, she believes Polyneices deserves a proper burial. Creon ignores her pleas. She brings Ismene outside the palace hoping she will help Antigone bury her fallen brother. However, Ismene refuses because she is worried she will be put to death for disobeying the king. Antigone disowns her sister and ventures out to find her brother's body.

Creon learns from a soldier that Polyneices has been buried against his orders. Outraged, Creon demands the culprit to be found.

The soldier returns with Antigone and she confesses that she buried her brother. Ismene falsely admits to helping Antigone, hoping that it will halve her punishment. Creon decides to have the sisters imprisoned.

Creon's son, Haemon is engaged to Antigone and he begs his father to reconsider his actions. Creon ignores his son and Haemon says he renounces his father.

After some consideration, Creon decides to spare Ismene. However, he has decided to bury Antigone alive in a cave. As Antigone is taken away to her tomb, the blind prophet, Tiresias enters. Tiresias begs Creon to bury Polyneices. If he does not, he will experience a foul punishment from the gods. Creon accuses Tiresias of being disrespectful to the king and disregards his warning.

Tiresias warns Creon that he will lose a son if he does not undo his actions. Creon knows that Oedipus, the former king, ignored Tiresias and he suffered greatly. Worried that he will suffer a similar fate, he agrees to free Antigone and give Polyneices a respectable burial.

As Creon is about to leave, a messenger informs him that his son, Haemon has committed suicide. Creon's wife, Eurydice enters and asks the messenger to tell her the exact circumstances of her son's death. The messenger tells her that Antigone hanged herself. When Haemon saw his fiancée dead, he stabbed himself.

Shocked, Eurydice runs into the palace. Creon runs out to collect Haemon's body. He returns, holding Haemon and acknowledges that he is responsible for his son's death.

Another messenger enters to inform Creon that Eurydice has killed herself. With her final breath, she cursed Creon. Creon blames himself and is left a broken man. He asks his servants to help him back into the palace.

5.
<u>Medea</u>
by Euripides
431 BC

A powerful sorceress seeks vengeance on her cheating husband after he leaves and humiliates her.

After the Greek hero, Jason has returned from his quest for the legendary Golden Fleece, he settles in Corinth. Here he marries a sorceress called Medea. They have two sons and are happy for many years.

Medea is the daughter of the wicked goddess of magic, Circe. Because of her relationship with the evil Circe, the Corinthians believe Medea to be wicked. Over the years, Jason realizes that associating with her is diminishing his legendary status.

Jason decides he can elevate his position among the Corinthians by leaving Medea for Glauce, daughter of King Creon (This is the same Creon from the play, Antigone. This story takes place years later.)

A nurse overhears Medea being distraught and she worries what the sorceress is going to do to herself or to her children.

Creon assumes Medea will seek revenge against his daughter, Glauce, so he intends to banish her. Medea pleads to Creon to let her stay one more day. The king agrees.

Jason meets Medea and apologises to her for betraying her. Jason said that he couldn't say no to a princess but he would like to keep Medea as his mistress. Medea is outraged by Jason's utter lack of respect to her. Medea reminds him that she left her family for him, had his children and saved him from a dragon. Jason promises to look after her after he marries Glauce. Medea promises that she will have her vengeance upon him.

Medea encounters the King of Athens, Aegeus. He voices how upset he is that he cannot have children.

Medea tells Aegeus of her situation and promises to give him a potion that will undo his infertility. In return, she asks Aegeus to allow her to live in Athens. He accepts her proposal.

Medea decides to murder Glauce and Creon by poisoning their golden robes that they intend to wear for the wedding. To make sure her vengeance against Jason comes full circle, Medea vows to kill her own children. Medea believes that the pain she will feel over the loss of her two boys will be overshadowed by her joy at watching Jason lose everything he ever loved.

She meets with Jason and pretends to apologise for her behavior earlier. She pleads to Jason to let her give Glauce the golden robes. Medea tells Jason that she hopes that this kind gesture will make Creon allow her children to stay in Corinth after she is banished. Jason accepts her terms and he lets his children deliver the robes to Glauce.

When Glauce put on the robes, she dies soon after. Creon finds his dead daughter and clutches her so tightly, he absorbs the poison and dies.

By the time Jason confronts Medea for killing his fiancée and the king, he learns that she has successfully killed his children as well.

Medea appears in the chariot of her grandfather, the Sun God, Helios. She looks upon Jason and tells him that she will take his sons away so he will never hold them in his arms again.

She escapes Corinth and finds sanctuary in Athens.

6.
<u>Oedipus the King</u>
by Sophocles
429 BC

A king does everything in his power to prevent a prophecy coming true that claims that he will kill his father and marry his mother.

This story takes place before Antigone and Medea. The play begins with the Theban people asking their king, Oedipus to help them eradicate a plague. Oedipus sends his brother-in-law, Creon to ask the oracle, Delphi for help. Creon believes the plague is a punishment since the last king, Laius was murdered and his killer has yet to be caught.

Oedipus beckons the blind prophet, Tiresias. Tiresias knows the answers to Oedipus' question but insists that the king abandon his quest. Oedipus accuses the prophet of having allegiance to the murderer but the prophet claims that Oedipus himself is the killer.

Oedipus dismisses this and assumes Tiresias was paid by Creon to mock him. Tiresias eventually leaves, mumbling that the murderer will be "a son and husband to his own mother."

Oedipus confronts and accuses Creon for forcing Tiresias to undermine the king. Oedipus sentences Creon to death.

Oedipus' wife and the daughter of the murdered king, Jocasta enter. She tells Oedipus not to listen to prophets because an oracle told Laius that his son would murder him. She knows this is not true because Laius was murdered by bandits at a crossroads.

Oedipus becomes curious about this fact and asks her to describe Laius to him. As she does, Oedipus becomes terrified. He explains to Jocasta that years ago he lived in Corinth. One day, a drunk accused Oedipus of not being his father's son. Perplexed by such a contradictory remark, he asked Delphi the oracle to elaborate. Delphi told Oedipus that he would "murder his father and sleep with his mother." To prevent this from ever happening, he left Corinth forever.

On his travels, a carriage nearly ran him off the road. He got into an argument with the carriagemen and killed them. Oedipus realizes that one of the men he killed must have been Laius.

A messenger arrives from Corinth to tell Oedipus that his father, Polybus has died. Oedipus is overjoyed because if his father has just died now, then the prophecy can't be true that he killed his father.

He is still worried that the prophecy might come true about him sleeping with his mother, Merope. The messenger puts his mind at ease by informing him that Merope is not his real mother. He clarifies that Merope and King Polybus adopted a baby that Laius abandoned. Jocasta had given orders to the messenger to have the child killed to prevent the prophecy that "the child would kill his father." Instead of killing the child, it was given to Merope.

Now Oedipus realizes that the prophecy has come true and he has killed his father and slept with his mother. Upon this revelation, Jocasta hangs herself and Oedipus tears out his own eyes so he won't have to look at his parents in the underworld when he dies.

Creon consults the oracles on what is to happen next. Oedipus' daughters, Antigone and Ismene are set to take control now that Oedipus is gone mad and blind. He warns them that they are part of a cursed family. Oedipus chooses to go into exile. Creon hopes he will not share a similar fate.

7.
__Electra__
by Sophocles
404 BC

Orestes needs to learn if his sister, Electra is still loyal to him after he learns that his mother has killed his father.

Orestes returns to his home city of Mycanae after many years. His friend, Pylades and his teacher, known only as the Old Man, accompany him.

Orestes is the son of Agamemnon who has been murdered by Orestes' mother, Clytemnestra, so she could be with her lover, Aegisthus. Orestes vows to kill his mother and the new king but before he does, he needs to verify if his sister, Electra is still loyal to him.

Orestes has a plan to discover if his sister is loyal. Many years have passed so Orestrd assumes she probably won't recognize him. He and Pylades intend to tell the Mycanaens that Orestes died in a chariot accident and they will see how the people react.

To completely sell the idea that Orestes is dead, they carry an urn pretending that his remains lie within. Orestes believes that when Electra sees the urn carrying what she believes to be the remains of her brother, she will not be able to hide her genuine feelings about him.

He visits his father's grave and leaves a lock of his hair on the tombstone.

Orestes doesn't know that Electra is devastated that her mother, Clytemnestra killed her father, Agamemnon. She runs outside and howls at the heavens in bereavement over her murdered father. Her younger sister, Chrysothemis emerges from the palace to see Electra in grief. She tells Electra that Aegisthus intends to lock her up if she doesn't be quiet. Chrysotemis leaves to visit her father's grave.

Clytemnestra enters and argues with Electra about her inability to get over her deceased father.

The Old Man appears and tells Clytemnestra that Orestes is dead. When Electra hears this, she is devastated. Clytemnestra shows her hospitality to the Old Man and invites him in.

When Chrysthemis notices a lock of Orestes' hair on Agamemnon's grave, she realizes that he is alive. She tries to tell Electra that her brother still lives but her sister is too rattled to listen. Electra is preparing to kill Clytemnestra.

Orestes enters Electra's chamber, carrying the urn. It has been so long that Electra doesn't recognize her brother. He tells her that the urn harbours her brother's remains. He hands her the container and she weeps for her fallen sibling. Only then does Orestes realize that Electra's loyalty towards him has never faltered. He reveals that he is Orestes.

He validates this further by showing her his father's ring.

Pylades reminds her that she must hide her joy in order to avoid suspicion from Clytemnestra. The Old Man enters and tells Orestes that now is the time to murder his mother. Orestes and Pylades enter the palace and kill Clytemnestra.

Her husband, Aegisthus returns home. Orestes covers Clytemnestra's dead body with a sheet and he presents it to Aegisthus and pretends that it is the body of Orestes. Aegisthus pulls off the sheet to reveal his murdered wife.

Orestes reveals his identity before slaying Aegiethus in the same location in which Clytemnestra murdered her last husband, Agamemnon. His father has been avenged.

8.
Brothers Menaechemus
by Plautus
Approx. 170 BC

A man gets mistaken for his long-lost twin, which creates many misunderstandings.

Moschus had twin sons, Menaechmus and Sosicles. Moschus took Menaechmus with him when he was a young child on a trip, leaving Sosicles with his grandfather in Syracuse.

While Moschus is on his trip, Menaechmus is abducted and adopted by a man from Epidamnus. When Moschus discovers this, he dies of a broken heart.

The grandfather changes Sosicles' name to Menaechmus to commemorate his brother's memory.

When the twins become men, Menaechmus seeks out his brother. He approaches Epidamnus, unaware that his sibling, Sosicles lives there. As Menaechmus approaches Epidamnus, Sosicles is leaving his house after having a quarrel with his wife.

Sosicles tells his friend, Peniculus that he has taken his wife's jewel and he is going to give it to his neighbour, Erotium, whom he has been having an affair with.

When Sosicles presents Erotium with his gift, he says that she should thank him with dinner. Erotium agrees and the two men go for a drink as she prepares the meal.

Menaechmus arrives in town with his slave, Messenio. Erotium sees Menaechmus and assumes he is Sosicles. She asks if he is ready for his meal. He sees the opportunity to have a free meal so he accepts her invitation. The next day, Erotium tells Menaechmus that the jewellery he gave her earlier doesn't fit her and he needs to have it re-sized. He accepts the jewellery with every intention of keeping it for himself.

He then bumps into Peniculus. Peniculus rants at Menaechmus for eating Erotium's meal without him. He vows to tell his wife about the jewellery he stole from her before storming off. Menaechmus is confused that people he has never met know his name.

Learning of his misdeeds, Sosicles' wife confronts him and orders him to have her jewellery returned to her. He goes to Erotium and asks for the jewellery but is perplexed when she tells him that she already gave it to him.

Sosicles' wife sees Menaechmus and assumes it is her husband. She asks if he is ashamed of himself. He says he doesn't know who she is. Outraged, she calls her father. As her father enters, Menaechmus pretends to go insane which scares him away.

As Menaechmus leaves the area, Sosicles enters. Sosicles' father-in-law re-enters with a doctor and they try to restrain Sosicles.

Messenio sees the men grabbing Sosicles and rescues him, believing him to be his master. For protecting his master from harm, Messenio asks for his freedom. Disorientated, Sosicles grants it. Messenio promises to return the money that he was safeguarding for his master. As he runs off, Sosicles goes to Erotium's house to reclaim the jewellery he gave her earlier.

Menaechmus walks into the area thar Sosicles was in moments before. Messenio enters to give his master his money. When Messenio tells Menaechmus that his master has just freed him a moment before, Sosicles questions his own mental state.

Suddenly, Sosicles leave's Erotium's house and sees his twin brother. They realize why there have been so many misunderstandings and they embrace each other. They decide to live together and Sosicles officially frees Messenio from slavery.

9.
The Aeneid
by Virgil
19 BC

The fall of Troy compels the young Trojan, Aeneas to begin his epic conquest to form the city of Rome.

This is the sequel to The Iliad and The Odyssey. Prince Aeneas is a cousin of Hector who Achilles killed in The Iliad. When Troy was being destroyed, Aeneas was saved by the goddess of love and his mother, Venus.

Wait a minute… In The Iliad, Aphrodite was the goddess of love. Who's Venus?

The Greeks called their goddess of love, Aphrodite but this story is Roman. In Ancient Rome, Aphrodite is called Venus, Zeus is called Jupiter, and his messenger, Hermes, is called Mercury. Now that has been cleared up, let's get back to the story.

With the city of Troy in ruins, Aeneas commandeers a fleet and sails the world in search for a new home. He makes his way to the city of Carthage. When he arrives in Carthage, Queen Dido greets him. At a banquet, he tells stories of how Troy was destroyed by the Greeks. Near the end of the Trojan War, Ulysses the Greek (the Roman name for Odysseus) created a huge wooden horse with the Greeks inside of it.

They left it outside the Trojan walls with only one Greek soldier called Sinon to tell the Trojans that the Greeks had fled. The Greeks pretended to sail away in defeat and the colossal horse was a gift from the gods.

The Trojan priest, Laocoon found the wooden horse suspicious. Sadly, no one listened to Laocoon and the Trojans happily brought the wooden horse through the fortified walls of Troy.

At nightfall, the Greeks within the horse burst out and started to destroy the city and kill the Trojans while they slept.

The ghost of Hector appeared to Aeneas and compelled him to flee. Aeneas is told by the king's daughter, Helenus that he is destined to find Italy and his future descendants will one day rule the world. Aeneas' wife, Creusa is killed in the Trojan War and her ghost tells Aeneas to find a new home.

On his journey, Aeneas and his crew nearly get sucked into Charybdis the whirlpool. The whirlpool hurls their ship onto the island of Polyphemus the Cyclops. This is the same island that Ulysses escaped from after he blinded the Cyclops. They met one of Ulysses' men who was still trapped on the island. They rescued him before the Cyclops attacked them.

As Aeneas finishes his tale, Dido realizes that she has fallen in love with him.

At first, Aeneas likes the idea of settling in Carthage but Jupiter's messenger, Mercury reminds him that he must venture onward to Italy,

As he leaves Carthage, he sees a huge funeral pyre. He realizes that it is for Dido who killed herself from a broken heart.

One night, Aeneas sees a vision of his dead father. He tells Aeneas that he must go to the underworld to see what the future of Rome is. When he arrives there, his father appears and shows him what lies in store for Rome. This spurs Aeneas to finish his quest.

He lands in the site of the future Rome, Lathium. He meets the daughter of King Latinus, Lavinia. The ruler of the neighbouring town, Turnus was intending to wed Lavinia. He challenges Aeneas to fight.

Aeneas kills Turnus, marries Lavinia and becomes the ruler of Rome.

10.
<u>Beowulf</u>
by Anon
1025

The oldest English story in existence tells of the warrior, Beowulf, who protects a kingdom from the monster, Grendel.

Hrothgar is the Danish king and rules from his great hall of Heorot. He celebrates at night with music and singing. The noise from the celebration enrages a troll called Grendel. The monster breaks into the king's hall, killing and devouring many people. Hrothgar's greatest warrior, Aeschere attacks the beast but even he cannot slay the demonic creature.

A great hero from Geatland called Beowulf hears of Hrothgar's plight and seeks him out. Beowulf desires to kill Grendel to give himself a legendary reputation. As he enters Heorot, one cynical warrior called Unferth believes that Beowulf exaggerates his achievements and believes he is not strong enough to defeat the monster.

Beowulf spends the night in Heorot and pretends to be asleep while waiting for Grendel to make his attack. The creature invades the great hall once more and kills many of Beowulf's men. Beowulf launches himself at the troll and rips off its arm. Grendel runs back to his mother in agony.

As the people of Heorot celebrate the following night, Grendel's Mother invades the hall and kills Hrothgar's prized soldier, Aeschere. Beowulf and his men track Grendel's Mother to her lair under a lake. Unferth gives Beowulf a powerful sword and apologises for doubting him earlier. Beowulf encases himself in armour to prepare for a fight to the death with this creature.

Beowulf swims into the lake until he reaches her lair. Once he arrives, Grendel's Mother immediately attacks him. She cannot hurt him because of his thick armour. His sword proves useless against Grendel's Mother, so he discards it.

Beowulf sees a magical sword from among the monster's treasure. He grabs it and swiftly decapitates her. He explores the lair to find a gravely injured Grendel. Beowulf quickly slays the beast. When the blade touches Grendel's poisonous blood, it melts the sword until only the hilt remains.

He brings the handle of the sword and Grendel's head out of the cave back to Heorot to show his victory to Hrothgar. Beowulf returns home to Geatland and becomes a king to his people.

Half a century after his battle with Grendel, a dragon invades Beowulf's kingdom and burns everything in sight because its treasure has been stolen. After a failed attempt to kill the dragon, Beowulf says that he will find its lair and kill it himself. His servant, Wiglaf refuses to leave his side and joins Beowulf to hunt the dragon down. They eventually find its lair at Earnaenaes. Beowulf is injured in the battle with the dragon but successfully slaughters it. He dies shortly after due to his wounds.

After Beowulf perishes, a huge funeral pyre is built to commemorate his memory.

11.
<u>1001 Arabian Nights</u>
by Various Authors
1300

A newlywed queen tells her tyrannical husband 1,001 stories in an effort to delay her execution.

Shahryar the Persian king is outraged when he discovers that his wife has been unfaithful to him and so, has her beheaded.

He convinces himself that all women are just as bad. He decides to wed a new bride every day, sleep with her that night, and have her executed the following morning so she cannot cheat on him.

After three years, the king's advisor, Jafar starts to have great difficulty obtaining new brides for the king.

Eventually, his own daughter, Scheherezade puts herself forward to marry the king. Jafar pleads for her not to go forward with it as he fears for her life. But Scheherezade is sick of the needless killing and she has a plan that she is certain will successfully end the bloodshed.

Her father relents and lets Scheherezade marry Shahryar. On the night of their wedding, Scheherezade tells her newlywed husband an incredible story. Shahryar is utterly captivated by the tale and it retains his undivided attention throughout the night.

This tale goes on for hours but just before she reaches the story's conclusion, the sun comes up. Scheherezade promises that she will finish the story the following night. Curious to see how the story ends, the king postpones her execution.

That night, Scheherezade finishes the story but as soon as it ends, she begins a new tale. As before, this story goes on all night. Dawn breaks before it ends. Shahryar has to wait another night to hear the conclusion.

For nearly three years, Scheherezade tells her husband every type of story under the sun – comedies, tragedies, historical tales, poems, and love stories. Her stories involve magical plants, talking animals, djinns, pirates, demons, ghosts, sea monsters, and wizards.

It is in these stories where we learn of iconic characters such as Sinbad the sailor, Ali Baba and the 40 Thieves, and the Chinese boy, Aladdin who finds a magical lamp that will grant him three wishes.

After 1,001 nights, Scheherezade says to the king, "My beloved, I have borne three children for you these past three years. Is that enough evidence to show that I would never hurt you?"

Shahryar realizes that he was wrong about punishing women. He forgives all womankind and embraces his wife and says he will always trust her.

12.
Doctor Faustus
by Christopher Marlowe
1592

An arrogant and unsatisfied doctor sells his soul to the devil in exchange for great power.

The play revolves around a lower-class worker called Faustus who educates himself until he becomes a doctor. Faustus eventually believes he has learned all he can be taught by man and craves more knowledge.

He asks his servant, Wagner to invite over two magicians called Valdes and Cornelius. When he asks them about mastering magic, the pair urge him not to, concerned that he will study the dark arts.

Over time, Valdes and Cornelius see Faustus less and less. They worry he's obsessing over black magic. They are correct in their suspicions for Faustus quickly becomes accustomed to summoning the forces of Hell. He conjures up a demonic servant of Lucifer called Mephistopheles.

Faustus can't gaze upon him because the demon looks so repulsive. The doctor demands that Mephistopeheles change into a friar. When Mephistopheles transforms into a human, Faustus feels proud that a demon obeyed him.

He commands Mephistopheles to serve him. The demon reminds the doctor that he only serves Lucifer. Mephistopheles also notifies him that it was the scripture that summoned him, not Faustus himself. Anyone who recites the scripture as Faustus had done allows Lucifer to claim the person's soul.

Faustus uses Mephistopheles to make a deal with Lucifer. Faustus asks for 24 years on Earth with Mephistopheles as his servant. After that, Faustus will be banished to Hell.

The bond must be made in blood. Faustus cuts himself and sees his wound instantly healed. Upon his wound are the words, "Homo, fuge! Which is Latin for "Flee, man!" Despite this warning, Faustus goes ahead with the deal believing that he is already damned.

Faustus wants to know all of the knowledge in existence but when he quizzes Mephistopheles about science, the demon is vague and dismissive. This frustrates Faustus as he feels like he gave up his soul for nothing.

A good angel and a bad angel appear to Faustus. The good angel pleads with Faustus to revoke his arrangement with Lucifer.

The bad angel spurs Faustus to continue with his pact with the Devil. Faustus discards the good angel's plea, believing he is beyond redemption.

Lucifer presents Faustus with people who encapsulate The Seven Deadly Sins but even this doesn't deter him.

With his new power, Faustus plays pranks on people whom he believes have wronged him in the past. He belittles his rivals by making them sprout antlers, stealing their food, or turning their horses into bundles of hay.

Faustus enjoys his power at first but, as time passes, becomes more self-conscious that he will suffer in hell for all eternity.

With one hour left before he is cast into Hell, Faustus repents and desperately pleads to God or Lucifer to save his soul. His request is ignored and the play ends with Faustus being dragged to Hell.

13.
A Midsummer Night's Dream
by William Shakespeare
1596

Lovers' lives are complicated by a fairy feud.

The play revolves around the wedding of the Amazon Queen, Hippolyta and Theseus of Athens. Their celebration takes place in a Fairyland realm.

Two men called Lysander and Demetrius are in love with Hermia. Her father, Egeus arranges for her to marry Demetrius but she only loves Lysander. Egeus forces a law on Theseus, stipulating that a daughter must marry the man her father chooses or she must face death.

Quince and his acting troupe are preparing a play about Pyramus and Thisbe to present after the wedding of Theseus and Hippolyta. The actor, Bottom, is to play the lead role, Pyramus. Bottom is arrogant and demands that he plays all of the main characters simultaneously.

The play shifts to a separate story about fairies. Oberon the Fairy King and his queen, Titania enter a nearby forest. Oberon requests Titania's attendant while she visits Hippolyta's wedding but she refuses to give her attendant to him.

Enraged, Oberon commands his trickster elf, Puck to create a juice from a magical flower. This juice will make anyone fall in love with the first person they see if it is poured into the person's eyes. Oberon pours the magical juice on Titania's eyes, hoping to humiliate her, believing she will fall in love with a forest animal.

Hermia and Lysander have run away to the forest, preparing to elope. Helena is desperate for Demetrius to be with her so she tells him that Hermia has eloped. He rejects her cruelly. Oberon sees this and orders Puck to use the flower on Demetrius to make him love Helena. Puck mistakes Lysander for Demetrius and sprays the magical juice onto Lysander as he sleeps. When he awakes, he sees Helena and instantly falls in love with her.

Recognizing Puck's blunder, Oberon places the spell on Demetrius himself. But after Demetrius awakens, he sees Helena, and is in love with her too. Their love is so over-the-top, Helena believes the men are mocking her. Hermia is jealous that Helena is getting the attention now. A fight between the two girls and two men ensues.

Oberon has to intervene and he removes the charm over Lysander.

Quince and his troupe move to the forest to do a rehearsal for their play. Puck spots Bottom. Knowing that "bottom" is another word for ass (as in "donkey,") Puck transforms Bottom's head into that of a jackass.

When Bottom enters his scene, the actors run in terror. Bottom is confused as he is oblivious of his transformation. Waiting for the actors to return, he sings out of boredom. His singing awakens Titania. When she sees Bottom, Titania instantly falls in love with him. While she is occupied with Bottom, Oberon takes her attendant. Satisfied he got what he wanted, Oberon asks Puck to restore Bottom back to normal and to make Hermia, Helena, Demetrius, and Lysander believe that everything that occurred to them was all a dream.

The fairies vanish while Theseus and Hippolyta enter and awaken the lovers. Theseus rejects Egeus' demands and decides to have a group wedding with Lysander marrying Hermia and Demetrius marrying Helena.

Bottom and his group perform their play. It's not very good because the group didn't have time to rehearse. Everyone at the wedding then goes to bed. Oberon, Titania, Puck, and other fairies enter while everyone sleeps and they bless the guests.

14.
<u>Romeo and Juliet</u>
by William Shakespeare
1597

Two lovers from rival families form a doomed relationship.

The play starts with servants from the Montague and Capulet families fighting each other in Verona. Prince Escalus stops the brawl under the threat of death.

Later, Count Paris asks Capulet if he may marry Capulet's daughter, Juliet. Capulet says she is too young but invites him to a ball. Juliet's nurse and mother try to convince Juliet to accept Paris' offer.

Later, Benvolio is speaking to his cousin, Romeo (who is Montague's son) about his depression. Romeo says he's upset because a girl called Rosaline who isn't interested in him. Benvolio and Romeo's friend, Mercutio convince him to go to the ball where he can win over Rosaline.

But at the ball, Romeo meets and falls for Juliet. Juliet's cousin, Tybalt threatens to kill him once he realizes that Romeo has sneaked into the ball uninvited. Juliet's father stops Tybalt from assaulting Romeo saying he doesn't want any more blood spilt.

After this, Romeo overhears Juliet talking to herself about how she loves him in spite of her family's vendetta against his family. He reveals himself and the two elope.

Friar Laurence believes their marriage can end the family feud and agrees to wed them the following day.

Tybalt is still furious that Romeo wasn't punished for sneaking into the ball and so challenges him to a duel. Romeo now sees Tybalt as his family and refuses to fight him. Ashamed that Romeo's cowardice will damage his family's name, Mercutio fights Tybalt in Romeo's place but he is stabbed and killed. Romeo retaliates by slaughtering Tybalt.

Romeo is banished from Verona under penalty of death. Romeo goes to Juliet's bedchamber and they sleep together.

Capulet, not knowing of Juliet's marriage, declares that she must marry Paris. When she rejects the proposal, Capulet threatens to disown her.

She asks Friar Laurence for help and he offers a potion that will put her in a deathlike coma for "two and forty hours."

Laurence vows to send a messenger to Romeo to make him aware of the plan so he can return to her when she awakes. She takes the potion and falls into a deathlike sleep. When her "body" is discovered, it is placed in a family crypt.

Romeo learns of Juliet's "death" from his servant before the messenger reaches him. He buys a poison and plans to drink it as soon as he sees his dead wife.

As he enters the crypt, Paris is there mourning Juliet. Paris believes he is there to vandalize the tomb and so, attacks him but Romeo kills him. Romeo then drinks the poison and dies. Juliet awakens from her coma and on seeing Romeo's body, stabs herself to death.

Both families meet in the crypt to find the bodies. Laurence tells them the whole story. Realizing that the tragedy was a huge misunderstanding, the families agree to end their feud.

15.
<u>Hamlet</u>
by William Shakespeare
1599

Prince Hamlet learns that his father is murdered and his mother has married her brother-in-law, who happens to be the murderer.

The Danish prince, Hamlet is depressed that his mother, Gertrude married his uncle, Claudius so soon after her husband's death.

Later, Hamlet's friends, Marcellus and Horatio tell him that they saw his father's ghost the previous night. That night, Hamlet sees the ghost and confirms it is his father. The ghost tells Hamlet that Claudius murdered him by pouring poison in his ear and he must be avenged. To avoid suspicion from Claudius, Hamlet feigns madness as he forms evidence against his father's killer.

Hamlet's girlfriend, Ophelia is worried that he doesn't love her. She tells her father, Polonius and her brother, Laertes of her concerns. They warn her off him saying he is not suitable for her. When Ophelia meets Hamlet, she doesn't realize that he's feigning madness. She becomes terrified of his unpredictable behaviour and tells her father. Polonius assumes Hamlet has gone mad because she didn't return his love.

Hamlet learns that a troupe of actors are coming to the castle. He has the idea to make the actors re-enact his father's murder and determine if Claudius is guilty based on his reaction. When they perform the play, the king suddenly leaves after he sees the poisoning scene performed the same way Claudius committed the murder.

Hamlet sees Claudius in a room praying to God for forgiveness for slaying his brother. Hamlet has a sword ready but feels he cannot kill a man when he is in prayer, believing that Claudius' soul would go to heaven.

Hamlet enters his mother's bedchamber and the two get into a heated argument. Hamlet is disgusted that she would sleep with another man so soon after his father's death. She becomes increasingly scared of him and she cries out for help. Polonius (who is hiding behind a curtain) cries out for help too. Hamlet assumes the person behind the curtain must be Claudius and stabs the curtain, killing Polonius.

Claudius sends Hamlet to England with two attendants, Rosencrantz and Guildenstern. They have instructions in sealed letters to have Hamlet sentenced to death. Hamlet switches the letters before the two men have a chance to read them. The new letters say that they are to be put to death. He also writes to Claudius saying that he is returning.

Ophelia goes mad after losing her father and drowns herself. Laertes is enraged that Hamlet has caused the death of his father and sister.

Claudius organizes a fencing match between the two. Laertes' sword will be poisoned, ensuring Hamlet's death. If that fails, Claudius will congratulate Hamlet with poisoned wine. When Hamlet returns, the fencing match begins. The poisoned blade stabs Hamlet but the two men drop their swords during the fight and pick up each other's weapon. Hamlet then stabs Laertes with the poisoned tip.

As a toast to her son, Hamlet's mother drinks the poisoned wine intended for Hamlet, killing her. As Laertes dies from the poisoned sword, he confesses about Claudius' scheme. Hamlet stabs Claudius with the blade. He then makes him drink the poisoned wine, killing him. Hamlet dies immediately after.

The Norwegian king, Fortinbras enters to see all of the royal family dead. He claims the kingdom as his own.

16.
Julius Caesar
by William Shakespeare
1599

The conspiracy to assassinate Julius Caesar has irreparable consequences for Rome.

The Roman emperor, Julius Caesar is a friend of his army commander, Marcus Brutus. His people admire him but the senators are worried that he will turn the Roman republic into his own monarchy.

Cassius is trying to convince Brutus that Caesar is becoming a dictator. Cassius is secretly jealous of Caesar's power. Brutus is a nobleman so the plan to get rid of Caesar won't look so corrupt if Brutus is behind it. After enough manipulation, Brutus agrees with Cassius that Caesar must be stopped.

The people of Rome rejoice that Caesar has returned after defeating a Civil War rival. Two officials called Flavius and Marellus stop the people from celebrating, saying that Caesar only got rid of his rival so he would be unchallenged as emperor. Caesar discovers this and has the two men removed from office.

A fortuneteller warns Caesar to "beware the Ides of March (the 15th of March)" but he dismisses the prophecy. His friends and wife, Calpurnia worry for Caesar's fate but he arrogantly ignores them, believing himself to be invincible.

On the 15th of March, Caesar enters the Senate where the conspirators move in and stab him one by one. Brutus delivers the final blow.

The conspirators do not hide the fact that they killed the emperor from the Roman people to emphasize that they committed this grave act for the good of Rome and not for their own gain.

But one of the senators, Mark Antony sways the public opinion by reminding the crowd of the good that Caesar accomplished. He shows them the body of the emperor and declares that every Roman citizen was to inherit 75 drachmas upon his death. When he is done speaking, the crowd turns against the conspirators and they are banished from Rome.

A Triumvirate (Latin for three ruling men) replaces Caesar. It is made up of Lepidus, Mark Antony, and Caesar's nephew, Octavius.

Brutus learns that his wife, Portia has committed suicide because she can't live without her husband. Brutus prepares for a war with Mark Antony and Caesar's adopted son, Octavius.

That night, Caesar's ghost appears to Brutus and warns him that he will be defeated if he goes to war. Cassius and Brutus enter the battle smiling and holding hands, accepting that they will die.

Cassius dies that day but Brutus battles on. The following day, he realizes that he has no possible chance of winning. He takes his own life by running into the sword of one of his own men.

Antony says that Brutus was "the noblest Roman of them all" because he was the only person who murdered Caesar for the good of Rome rather than his own agenda.

17.
King Lear
by William Shakespeare
1609

A king is driven mad when he rewards his evil daughters and banishes the one daughter that truly loved him.

King Lear divides his kingdom between his daughters; Goneril and Regan, believing that they love him dearly. Little does he know that they manipulate him with fictitious affection. He banishes his other daughter, Cordelia, believing she doesn't love him even though she is the only one who has genuine love for her father. The Duke of Kent says that Lear is being unreasonable and he is also banished. The King of France admires Cordelia and marries her.

Gloucester introduces Kent to his bastard son, Edmund. Edmund hates the fact that he is known for his illegitimacy and intends to get rid of his brother, Edgar (who is Gloucester's actual son.) He forges a letter in Edgar's writing that details Edgar's intentions to steal his father's estate. When Gloucester reads the letter, he demands to speak to Edgar. Edmund tells Edgar to run away. As he does, Edmund cuts his own arm and tells Gloucester that Edgar is responsible. Gloucester banishes Edgar.

Kent returns from his banishment in disguise under the name, Caius. Lear hires him as a servant. The king then visits his daughters and realizes they don't love him. Furious, he wanders into a storm shouting how ungrateful his daughters are. Eventually, Lear meets Edgar, who pretends to be a lunatic called Tom. Kent finds shelter for all of them.

Edmund betrays Gloucester to Lear's evil daughters. He shows proof that Gloucester intends to reinstate Lear as king. Regan's husband, Cornwall gouges Gloucester's eyes out. A servant attacks Cornwall, fatally wounding him. Regan kills the servant and tells Gloucester that Edmund betrayed him and then forces Gloucester to wander outside alone and blind, assuming that he will succumb to a slow death. Edgar meets his blind father and cares for him with Gloucester oblivious that it is his son who is helping him. Gloucester wants to die so he asks "Tom" to lead him off a cliff to his death.

Goneril starts to see her husband, Albany as a coward and she falls for Edmund. Regan also loves Edmund and the sisters turn on one another.

Kent leads Lear to the French army, which is now commanded by Cordelia. Lear is half-mad at this point. To spite Goneril, Albany joins forces with the French.

Edgar pretends to lead Gloucester to a cliff that he can jump off. Edgar changes his voice and tells Gloucester that he survived the fall. Lear appears and it is clear that he is now completely deranged.

Goneril's servant, Oswald, appears and tries to kill Gloucester but is murdered by Edgar. In his pocket, Edgar finds Goneril's letter encouraging Edmund to kill Gloucester.

The British and the French engage in battle. Lear and Cordelia are captured. Edmund orders Cordelia to be executed. With the British being victorious, Regan announces that she will marry Edmund. Albany reveals Goneril's lust for Edmund. This is validated when Regan becomes ill, having been poisoned by Goneril. She is escorted away and dies. Edmund challenges Albany to combat. An unrecognizably armoured Edgar enters to fight Edmund on Albany's behalf. He delivers a fatal blow to Edmund. Goneril flees and commits suicide. Edgar reveals himself and announces that Gloucester died earlier of shock when he learned Edgar was still alive and he was in fact the man who was helping him.

Lear enters, carrying Cordelia's corpse. Albany tells Lear that he shall be reinstated as king but he dies of a broken heart. Edgar is made king.

18.
<u>Othello</u>
by William Shakespeare
1603

Iago pretends to befriend Othello to destroy his life and fulfil his own end.

The play begins with Roderigo complaining to a soldier called Iago. Roderigo is infatuated with a woman called Desdemona but he has learned that she has secretly married a dark-skinned Venetian general. He is known as Othello the Moor.

Iago despises Othello for promoting a man called Cassio to a position he himself craved. Iago also believes that Othello slept with his wife, Emilia.

He begins to plot his revenge against the Venetian. He tells Desdemona's father, Senator Brabantio, about Desdemona's secret marriage.

He then finds Othello and warns him that the senator is onto him. Before Brabantio has a chance to punish Othello, word spreads that the Turks are invading Cyprus. Since Othello is the general, he begins making preparations. When Brabantio and Othello meet with the senators, Brabantio accuses the Moor of seducing his daughter.

He defends himself and Brabantio realizes that Othello truly loves Desdemona. The general leads his army to Cyprus only to find that a storm has destroyed the Turkish fleet. Othello celebrates by spending time with his wife privately.

While they are occupied, Iago gets Cassio drunk and forces Roderigo to pick a fight with him. After the brawl starts, Othello bursts in to put a stop to the brawl. He is disappointed by Cassio's behavior and relieves him of his rank.

Iago tells Cassio to speak to Desdemona to try and convince Othello to reinstate him. Iago tells Othello to be wary of Cassio and Desdemona spending time together.

Iago asks his wife, Emilia to take Othello's handkerchief. She does so, not asking why. Iago plants the handkerchief in Cassio's belongings. Othello realizes that it has gone missing and Iago tells him to watch Cassio to see if he acts suspiciously when Iago interrogates him about the handkerchief. Iago goes up to Cassio and asks him about a girl he has been seeing called Bianca. Othello is too far away to hear what the two men are saying. He assumes that when Cassio is referencing Bianca, he is talking about Desdemona. When this is happening, Bianca finds the handkerchief in Cassio's belongings and shouts at him for giving her a second-hand gift.

Othello is so enraged, he vows to kill his wife and tells Iago to murder Cassio. Roderigo complains to Iago that he has gained nothing in this plot. Iago convinces him to kill Cassio.

Roderigo tries to murder Cassio on the street but Cassio stabs him. In mid-fight, Iago cuts Cassio in the leg. Cassio doesn't see Iago's face and when he screams in agony, Iago appears, saying that he will help Cassio. Iago kills Roderigo to stop him revealing his evil scheme.

That night, Othello confronts and smothers Desdemona to death in bed. Emilia arrives and sees Othello over Desdemona's body and screams for help.

The governor arrives with Iago, Cassio, and others. Othello tells them that he knew his wife was unfaithful because of the handkerchief.

Emilia then realizes that Iago is responsible for the scheme. As she reveals that Iago has manipulated everything, Iago kills her.

Othello then stabs Iago (but not fatally.) To avoid being imprisoned for his wife's murder, Othello commits suicide with a hidden dagger. Iago is arrested.

19.
Don Quixote
by Miguel de Cervantes Saavedra
1605

After reading too many novels about knighthood, Don Quixote decides that he wants to have his own adventure.

The novel centres on a 50-year-old retired man called Alonso Quixano. He lives in La Mancha with his niece, his housekeeper, and a small boy.

The story centres on a man called Quixan. He keeps reading books about medieval knights and grows an obsession about it. He becomes so captivated by knighthood, he decides to go on a medieval adventure. He dons an old suit of armor, renames himself Don Quixote, and names his old horse, Rocicante. When he sees his beautiful neighbor, Aldonza, he renames her Dulcinea and imagines her as his lover. With his troop ready for adventure, Don Quixote, Rocicante, and Dulcinea begin their journey.

Don Quixote enters an inn (which he thinks is a castle) and demands that the innkeeper dub him a knight. He gets into a fight with some of the locals, so the innkeeper dubs him a knight just to get rid of him.

After that, Don finds a boy who is tied to a tree and frees him. Don discovers who the boy's master is and learns that he beats the boy. Don tells the master never to beat the child again. The master promises and Don leaves, feeling proud of his good deed. He doesn't realize that the boy is beaten immediately after he exits.

Don then encounters traders who insult his lover, Dulcinea. He attacks them but is beaten to a pulp. He returns home to recover.

As Don's wounds heal, his niece and housekeeper burn all of his books about knighthood and seal his library away.

When Don has recovered, he asks his other neighbor, Sancho to be his squire and promises to make him a governor of an island if he joins him on his adventure. Sancho accepts Don's invitation.

Don has many imaginary adventures with Sancho. He battles colossal giants (which are actually windmills) and fights shielded warlocks (which, in reality are pillow-wielding friars.) The friars he attacks were accompanying a lady. Now that Don has saved the lady from "the warlocks," he demands that all of her company submit to him.

Sancho and Don meet a bunch of goatherders. Don tells them of the old days where men didn't try to own as much land as possible and they just lived contentedly in peace. They invite Don to a funeral. The funeral is for a man who, much like Don, was obsessed with books about shepherds and fantasised about becoming one himself.

When they leave, Don and Sancho make their way through the woods. Riders stop near a lake so the ponies can have a drink. Don's horse, Rocinante tries to mate with one of the ponies so the men punch the poor horse. Don steps in to protect Rocinante but the men pummel him and Sancho.

Don meets many more colorful characters on his adventures but nearly all of it is in his head. If the people he encounters are real, he misinterprets their circumstances or greatly exaggerates about them.

Don is persuaded to return home by Sancho (mainly because Don keeps annoying people and getting hurt and Sancho always ends up feeling humiliated.)

20.
Macbeth
by William Shakespeare
1606

A noble warrior kills a king after hearing a prophecy that he will take the throne but he is driven mad with guilt.

The play begins with The Three Witches creating a magic spell. The next scene then switches to a Scottish warrior called Macbeth battling against the forces of Norway and Ireland. A sergeant informs them that the Thane of Cawdor has betrayed them and joined the enemy. Nevertheless, Macbeth's enemies surrender.

Shortly after, Macbeth and his ally, Banquo are visited by The Three Witches who call Macbeth the Thane of Glamis, the Thane of Cawdor, and the future king. He corrects them, saying he is only the Thane of Glamis.

The witches vanish as Macbeth's friend, Ross arrives to congratulate him on his new title as Thane of Cawdor. Macbeth realizes that if the Witches were correct about this, then their prophecy of him becoming king must be true.

King Duncan arrives and insists that he shall dine and stay at Macbeth's home to celebrate their victory.

Macbeth writes a letter about the Witches to his wife, Lady Macbeth. When Macbeth meets her, she convinces him that it is destiny that the king is staying in their home. All he has to do to become king is kill Duncan. As the king sleeps, Macbeth stabs him.

Macbeth's friends, Macduff and Lennox enter. Macduff discovers the body and is horrified. King Duncan's sons, Malcolm and Donalbain decide to flee, fearing for their lives. With no prince to claim the throne, Macbeth is made king.

Since Banquo was the only other person to witness the Witches' prophecy, Macbeth's paranoia starts to overwhelm him. He has Banquo assassinated.

Convinced that he got away with it, Macbeth has a banquet for his men. However, he keeps seeing the ghost of Banquo and starts screaming at him. His guests can only see Macbeth shouting at an empty chair.

Realizing that the Witches tricked him, he returns to them and asks them what the future has in store for him. They say he has nothing to fear as no one born from a woman can harm him. Macbeth thinks he cannot be killed since everybody is born from a woman.

Lennox appears and tells him that Macduff has fled to England. Macbeth orders the death of Macduff's entire family.

Lady Macbeth keeps imagining that there is blood on her hands. As she loses her mind, she desperately tries to wash the imaginary blood off her hands every night. She kills herself soon after, which barely affects Macbeth.

Macduff is told that his entire family has been killed. He vows revenge against Macbeth. King Duncan's son, Malcolm has formed an army to fight against the tyrant king, Macbeth.

Malcolm's forces battle against Macbeth's army. After slaying several men, the battle concludes with Macbeth confronting Macduff. Macbeth taunts Macduff by claiming that no man born of woman can kill him.

Macduff reveals that he wasn't "born of woman" since his mother had him via caesarean section. Macbeth is killed and Prince Malcolm becomes the rightful king.

21.
<u>Paradise Lost</u>
by John Milton
1667

After being banished from Heaven, Satan seeks vengeance on God by exposing mankind to Original Sin.

Lucifer was an angel in Heaven who believed God would choose him to be His second-in-command. However, God created an extension of Himself called the Son of God and Lucifer is not chosen to be God's servant.

Outraged, Lucifer and several angels declare war on God. After days of battle, the Son of God appears and singlehandedly defeats Lucifer and his army.

Lucifer and his rebel angels are cast out of Heaven and are banished to Hell where they are put in chains in a lake of fire.

Lucifer (who now calls himself Satan) frees himself from his shackles and forges a capital called Pandemonium. It is here where he decides to start building his army against God. His generals are Beezelbub, Mammon, Belial, and Moloch. Beelzebub concocts the idea of corrupting God's proudest creation – Humanity. He convinces Satan that he should expose mankind to Sin so that they would lose their purity. Satan loves this idea so much, he wishes to carry it out personally.

God suddenly becomes aware of Satan's intentions and he orders a council to discuss what he will do. The Son of God says that if Satan forces humanity to be exposed to Original Sin, the Son of God will convert to a human form and go to Earth and die for humanity's sins.

On his travels, Satan sees the angel of the sun, Uriel. Satan reverts to an angelic form and tells Uriel that he wishes to see mankind. Uriel allows Satan passage to Earth and he makes his way towards the Garden of Eden.

The Garden is inhabited by the first man and woman created by God, Adam and Eve. God allows them to do whatever they want except eat from the Tree of Knowledge.

Satan has become so corrupt that entering the Garden of Eden causes him pain. Uriel detects an impurity in the Garden. He realizes that Satan is evil and requests backup. The angel, Raphael finds Satan and banishes him from the Garden. He then tells Adam and Eve the story of how Lucifer fell from God's grace. Adam seems eager to know more and Raphael warns him that an insatiable thirst for knowledge can be destructive. There are some things that human beings should not know.

After eight days, Satan sneaks back into the Garden. He disguises himself as a snake and he speaks to Eve. She is astounded that a snake can talk. Satan tells her that he learned how to speak when he ate from the Tree of Knowledge. This convinces her to eat from it too.

Adam sees this and since Eve is bound to him since they were made together, he decides to eat from the tree too.

Adam and Eve obtain knowledge but they also obtain Original Sin. As a result, they experience shame, guilt, and fear for the first time.

They beg God for forgiveness but are banished from the Garden of Eden. The angel, Michael appears and shows them a vision. The vision reveals all of the horrific things that will happen to mankind and the vision concludes with The Great Flood wiping out most of humanity.

Adam is terrified of humanity's future but Michael reassures him that mankind can be redeemed from the sin that Adam and Eve inherited if the Son of God were to die for humanity.

22.
Robinson Crusoe
by Daniel Defoe
1719

A man finds himself marooned on an uncharted island and he attempts to adapt to the lifestyle.

In spite of his parents' pleas, Robinson Crusoe leaves England and sets sail on a sea journey. However, his ship is wrecked in a storm. He returns to land but intends to set sail again.

On his next sea journey, his ship is taken over by pirates and he is made their slave.

Two years later, he escapes in a small boat. A Portuguese captain rescues him and brings him onto his ship, which is sailing to Brazil. Because of his hardship, the captain helps Crusoe obtain a plantation.

Years pass and Crusoe joins an expedition crew, planning to bring slaves from Africa. But he is shipwrecked and lands on an island near Venezuela.

He is the sole survivor of the crew. From the wreckage, he finds tools and supplies. He builds a habitat near a cave. He forges a calendar, grows his own crops, hunts for meat, makes pottery, raises some goats and keeps a parrot as his pet. He reads the Bible and thanks God for sparing his life.

24 years after he is shipwrecked on the island, Crusoe discovers a footprint that is not his own. He learns that the island is the home of cannibals. The savages are capturing and imprisoning people to feast upon. At first, Crusoe wishes to kill them but then realizes that he can't. The cannibals are brutes but they are not evil. They are not intellectually aware of why their actions are immoral.

One evening, Crusoe stumbles upon the remains of a cannibal feast. He sees 30 cannibals making their way to the shore holding two victims. One victim is killed but the other one escapes and runs towards Crusoe's area. Crusoe and the victim attack the cannibals together. After the remaining cannibals flee, the victim demands to serve Crusoe. Crusoe dubs the man Friday, which is the day Crusoe arrived on the island many years ago.

Crusoe teaches him how to speak English and he converts Friday to Christianity. Friday longs to be reunited with his family. This concerns Crusoe because he doesn't want to lose his assistant.

Later, the duo find 20 cannibals guarding their victims. Crusoe and Friday kill the cannibals and save two prisoners; one is Friday's father and the other is a Spanish man. The Spaniard tells Crusoe that there are more Spaniards shipwrecked on the mainland.

They intend to go to the mainland with Friday's father, find the Spaniards, build a ship and sail back to Spain. They all head to Crusoe's dwelling. After they rest, Crusoe sends Friday's father and the Spaniard out in a canoe to explore a neighbouring island.

Shortly after, an English ship appears. A mutiny broke out on the ship and the mutineers decided to abandon their captain on the island. Crusoe takes the ship and leaves most of the mutineers on the island. He keeps five of the crew as hostages.

After months of sailing, Crusoe lands back in England. His family assumed he died a long time ago.

He heads to Portugal to obtain the profit from his estate in Brazil. He obtains a vast fortune and sends the money to England to avoid travelling by sea and it is divided among his family.

23.
Gulliver's Travels
by Jonathan Swift
1726

Upon Gulliver's travels, he encounters Lilliputians, giants, savages, immortals, and many more.

In 1699, a surgeon called Lemuel Gulliver is washed ashore after a shipwreck. He lands in Lilliput; a land inhabited by six-inch tall humans. The Lilliputians naturally fear him but Gulliver assures them he is not a monster so they accept him into their society.

His vast size comes in handy when the Lilliput King asks Gulliver to help them defeat their neighbors, Blefuscu. The king asks Gulliver to destroy the Blefuscans but he declines. The king accuses him of treason and authorizes him to be blinded. Gulliver flees and finds a boat. He sails out to sea, where a passing ship rescues him and takes him home. He learns that he's been away for three years.

A few months later, he sails out again and gets into another shipwreck. He washes up on Brobdingnag; a land inhabited by 70ft tall giants.

He is brought to the king and queen and they discuss the politics of their societies. The king is furious to learn that Europe uses weapons. Brobdingnag has no belief in wars, invasion, or poverty.

While he is being transported in a box, a gigantic eagle grabs Gulliver and takes him out to sea. He is rescued and brought home to learn that he was away for four years.

Gulliver sails out once again two months later. He is attacked by pirates and is marooned on an island until he is rescued by the inhabitants of the floating island of Laputa. Laputa is a kingdom that is devoted to music, arts, and maths but the inhabitants can't use them practically.

He visits the land below called Balnibarbi where the inhabitants are incapable of using science properly (They try to control sunbeams through cucumbers.)

Gulliver goes to Glubbdubdrib where a magician can resurrect historical figures. However, the magician sees his power as a gimmick rather than a way to learn from the past.

Gulliver visits Luggnagg where he meets immortals called Strudbrugs. The Strudburgs live forever but they aren't preserved in their age. They wither away into skeletal beings but never die. Gulliver leaves for home.

Realising that he's been away for four years and he has lost eleven years because of his travels, he decides to stay home.

As the months pass, he yearns for the sea and sets sail yet again with a crew. His crew devises a mutiny against Gulliver and abandons him near an island.

On this island, he meets a group of human savages and a race of horses called Houyhnhnms (Don't try to pronounce it.) The horses tell Gulliver that the savages are called Yahoos. They can't accept Gulliver because they think he is a Yahoo.

Gulliver rejects humanity, believing that humans are closer to the savagery of the Yahoos than the majesty of the Houyhnhnms.

He takes to the sea and is rescued. When he is taken back home, Gulliver believes that everyone he sees is a Yahoo and he rejects society. He completely neglects his children and his wife.

The book ends with Gulliver completely insane in a stable trying to speak to a horse.

24.
<u>Tom Jones</u>
Henry Fielding
1749

A wealthy squire finds that he must look after a newborn baby that has been abandoned in his home.

A rich Squire called Allworthy and his unmarried sister, Bridget live in a vast estate in Somerset.

After a long business trip in London, Allworthy returns home to find an abandoned baby sleeping in his bed. He beckons his housekeeper, Mrs. Deborah Wilkins to tend to the child. Allworthy seeks out the mother and father of the baby immediately.

Wilkins asks the people of the village for information about the child. She learns that a schoolmaster's servant called Jenny Jones is likely to be the mother. Jenny is brought to Wilkins and Allworthy and she admits that the baby is hers but she won't reveal the identity of the father. Allworthy assumes the father is Jenny's tutor, Partridge.

Allworthy brings Jenny to a different location to make sure the baby doesn't tarnish his reputation. He promises to care for the child who he names Thomas.

Two brothers called Dr. Blifil and Captain Blilfil routinely visit Allworthy's estate. The Captain eventually marries Bridget. He only marries her so he can attain Allworthy's wealth. Bridget and the Captain have a son (also called Blifil) who grows up with the bastard, Thomas.

As the Captain spends more time with his wife, he starts to neglect his brother. Over time, the Doctor moves out of the house and dies soon after, apparently from a broken heart.

The Captain seems to have a habit of giving everybody the cold shoulder as he starts to neglect his own wife. One day, the Captain goes for a walk and is found dead shortly after from a stroke.

The story skips forward 12 years. Tom grows up to be energetic, honest, and kind. He has two teachers, Square and Thwackum who detest Tom Jones. Many people hate Tom because he is a bastard but Allworthy loves him like his own son.

Tom grows fond of Molly; the a daughter of Allworthy's servant and gamekeeper, Black George. Tom and Molly develop a relationship and she falls pregnant, which urges Tom to marry her.

But Tom learns that Molly is promiscuous with other men and he decides that she is not the right woman for him. He becomes smitten with a neighbour's daughter, Sophia Western. However, Sophia's father is a squire and refuses to have his daughter associated with a bastard. He wants her to marry the third Blifil brother, Master Blifil, but she dismisses the idea.

While in London, Tom sleeps with two older women called Mrs. Waters and Lady Bellaston.

Eventually, it is revealed that Jenny Jones is actually Mrs. Waters. This means that Tom slept with his mother!

But that turns out to be untrue. Bridget is Tom's real mother. She fell pregnant after she slept with a schoolmaster. This means that Tom is the true nephew of Allworthy.

Allworthy decides to bestow nearly all of his inheritance on Tom. Tom marries Sophia and she bears a son and daughter and they all live happily ever after.

25.
Sense and Sensibility
by Jane Austen
1811

Mister Dashwood dies and his three daughters are left with no inheritance, changing their relationship forever.

Henry Dashwood and his second wife have three daughters – Marianne, Margaret, and Elinor. When Henry dies, he leaves all of his money to his first wife's son, John. This leaves the girls with no home or income.

They are asked to stay with distant cousins, the Middletons at Barton Park. Elinor is very upset about moving because she had become close to Edward Ferrars; the brother-in-law of her half-brother John (Try not to think about that too hard.)

As they move to Barton Park, Elinor and Marianne make many new friends. Two of their new acquaintances are bachelors – a retired officer called Colonel Brandon and the charming John Willoughby.

Marianne twists her ankle as she runs down a hill and Willoughby attends her injury, making her fall for him. They become close but then Willoughby suddenly announces that he is departing for London on business.

Lady Middleton discovers that she has two relatives she wasn't aware of called Anne and Lucy Steele. They quickly make themselves at home and Lucy informs Elinor that she has been engaged to Ferrars for a year. This news devastates and humiliates Elinor.

Marianne and Elinor make their way to London with Lady Middleton's mother, Mrs. Jennings. Brandon alerts Elinor that the people of London are gossiping about the engagement of Willoughby and Marianne. Marianne cannot wait to see Willoughby again but when she sees him at a party in town, he dismisses her. Later, he sends her a letter saying that he never loved her.

Brandon enlightens Elinor that Willoughby has a tendency to be cruel, sleazy, and bad with money. He has moved to London to marry a wealthy heiress called Miss Grey.

Anne Steele makes Lucy's engagement to Ferrars public knowledge. Out of anger, Ferrars' mother disinherits him.

The sisters leave London and visit family friends in Cleveland. Marianne develops a cold and becomes gravely ill. Hearing of her deteriorating health, Willoughby visits her, hoping that she will forgive him.

He explains to Elinor why he has treated her so cruelly. It turns out that he slept with Brandon's ward, got her pregnant, and left her. When his aunt learned of this fact, she cut off his inheritance. Without money, he became homeless and rushed off to London in a desperate attempt to marry someone wealthy. He tells Elinor that he truly loved Marianne but he couldn't be with her since he had no money. Elinor pities Willoughby and passes on his message to her ill sister. Learning of his confession, Marianne realizes that she could never have been happy with Willoughby. This allows her to get over him. Her health improves soon after.

The Dashwood family returns home and learns that Lucy is officially engaged to Ferrars.

However, Ferrars arrives in their home and tells Elinor that Lucy was only marrying him for his money. Once he was disinherited, she dumped him and became engaged to his brother, Robert. He proposes to Elinor and she accepts. Brandon becomes engaged to Marianne soon after.

26.
Pride and Prejudice
by Jane Austen
1813

Elizabeth Bennet falls for Mr. Darcy, but she is considered to be beneath his class. Will the two overcome their pride and prejudice?

The story begins with a rich bachelor called Charles Bingley moving into the neighborhood.

Mrs. Bennet is trying to find potential husbands for her five daughters – Elizabeth, Jane, Catherine, Mary, and Lydia.

Bingley is accompanied by his friend, Mr. Darcy who seems rude and sarcastic. Bingley meets Jane at a ball and becomes attracted to her. Jane talks to Elizabeth about her feelings for Bingley. Darcy seems quite taken by Elizabeth but she dismisses him.

Jane visits Bingley while he is visiting his sister, Caroline. Jane catches a cold and stays at his place. Elizabeth cares for her sister and is forced to put up with Darcy.

An heir to the Bennet household called Mr. Collins arrives at Elizabeth's home to choose a wife. At first, he chooses Jane, but because of her affection for Bingley, Mrs. Bennet nudges Collins to accept Elizabeth as his wife.

Elizabeth refuses and begins a friendship with an officer called Mr. Wickham. Wickham tells her how Darcy was rude to him in spite of Wickham being a godson to Darcy's father. This conversation makes Elizabeth like Darcy even less.

Shortly after, Collins proposes to Elizabeth but she isn't interested. Collins then proposes to Elizabeth's friend, Charlotte, and she accepts.

Bingley suddenly leaves for London, which devastates Jane. Elizabeth assumes it was Darcy's idea for Bingley to leave Jane.

That spring, Elizabeth meets Collins and Charlotte in Kent. She is invited to meet Darcy's aunt, Lady Catherine de Bourgh. Darcy confronts Elizabeth and confesses his love for her and asks for her hand in marriage. She refuses and accuses of him of being responsible for ruining Jane's relationship with Bingley.

Darcy writes a letter to Elizabeth in order to justify his crude behavior. In this letter, he writes how he genuinely did not believe Jane had any feelings for Bingley. Elizabeth realizes that she has misjudged Darcy.

Several months pass and Elizabeth, her aunt, and her uncle visit Darcy's home, assuming he will be out. Darcy unexpectedly returns and Elizabeth finds him pleasant and presentable, which she finds out of character. She starts to find him attractive. Suddenly, Elizabeth is alerted that her sister, Lydia has eloped with Wickham. She worries that this will bring shame upon her family and Darcy will no longer be interested in her.

Lydia and Wickham are located and they agree to have a conventional wedding.

Elizabeth, Jane, and their father discover that Elizabeth's uncle bribed Wickham to marry Lydia. Elizabeth discovers a letter that details how Darcy helped Wickham and Lydia get together.

Bingley suddenly asks for Jane's hand in marriage, which she accepts.

Lady Catherine arrives at Elizabeth's home. She has heard that Elizabeth is going to marry Darcy and she advises her not to because Catherine wants him to wed her daughter, Anne. Elizabeth is disgusted by this request. Catherine threatens her and says her marriage to Darcy will never happen.

When Elizabeth sees Darcy again, she thanks them for helping Lydia and Wickham get together. He proposes to her once more and this time, Elizabeth accepts.

27.
__Emma__
by Jane Austen
1815

A woman believes she's a good matchmaker until things fall apart for the couples she sets up.

Emma Woodhouse is a beautiful 20-year-old girl who lives in Surrey with her widowed father.

Emma has just attended the wedding of her friend, Mrs. Weston. Emma takes credit for getting the two together and convinces herself that she would be a great matchmaker.

Her neighbor and brother-in-law, George Knightley, advises against this idea (as he often does) but she ignores him. Emma decides to pair up her pretty but ditzy friend, Harriet with the vicar, Mr. Elton.

Because Emma is showing Mr. Elton attention, he believes that she is in love with him and so, he proposes to her. Emma says to Elton that she assumed he fancied Harriet. Elton becomes angry that Emma has the audacity to accuse him of liking someone like Harriet whom he considers socially inferior. Harriet is devastated when she learns of Elton's rejection. Emma realizes that she isn't cut out to be a matchmaker.

As time goes by, Elton marries a wealthy but vain woman who has mutual friends of Emma's which means she must put with her irritating behavior. The Eltons are very rude to Harriet at a dance. To stop her from being humiliated, George asks Harriet to dance with him.

A handsome gentleman called Frank Churchill arrives in the neighbourhood. He charms everyone except George who warns Emma to stay away from Frank.

An orphan called Jane Fairfax also enters the neighborhood. She is shy but beautiful and elegant. She is the niece of one of Emma's neighbours, Miss Bates. Jane is a musical prodigy and Miss Bates is very proud of her. Emma finds Jane's sudden appearance in the neighborhood suspicious. She tells Frank that she is suspicious of Jane and he agrees.

Frank and Emma flirt with each other but over time, she feels like Frank would be better suited to Harriet.

Emma wants her young nephew, Donwell to inherit George's family property.

Emma offends Miss Bates with a throwaway insult. George informs her that she has greatly upset Bates. Emma says she will apologise to her immediately. George is surprised by the fact that Emma has recognised she has done wrong. Jane becomes ill but she will not see Emma or accept her gifts. It is announced that she has accepted a position as governess by one of Elton's friends.

Shortly after this announcement, it is declared that Frank's aunt has died. It is discovered that Frank and Jane have been secretly engaged for the past year. Emma is stunned at how wrong she has been yet again.

Emma is worried that Harriet will be heartbroken but she is now in love with George. This shatters Emma's confidence even further when she acknowledges that she has been in love with George all along.

George tries to console Emma when he sees how upset she is. She makes her feelings known to him and he confesses that he is also in love with her. He proposes and she accepts.

A young farmer called Robert Martin proposes to Harriet. Robert was the man Harriet was going to marry before Emma convinced her to marry Elton. Harriet accepts the proposal and Emma and Jane reconcile.

28.
Frankenstein
by Mary Shelley
1818

A scientist resurrects a dead body, changing his life forever.

Captain Robert Walton is writing letters to his sister, Margaret, while he is exploring the North Pole. Robert is a failed writer and he believes exploration can broaden his insight to write. From the ship, his crew sees a large figure on a dog sled. Later, they rescue a freezing man called Victor Frankenstein. Victor tells them he was chasing the man Walton saw earlier. Victor can sense that Walton craves success and is full of ambition and so tells him a cautionary tale.

At university, Victor learned how to turn non-living matter into living matter. Over time, he attempted to create a fully-functioning living creature made from dead matter. He made a body out of human corpses and animal organs. Victor finds it difficult to attach smaller and more delicate body-parts, so he works with larger muscles and organs. As a result, the Creature is 8ft tall. When the Creature is brought to life (it's never explained how), Victor is so repulsed by its yellow skin and protruding muscles, he runs away. The Creature feels abandoned and flees in shame.

Victor becomes sick from the incident. His friend, Henry looks after him. Four months pass and Victor recovers. He returns home to discover that his little brother, William, has been murdered. Evidence points to William's nanny as the culprit but Victor sees the Creature that night and suspects it is responsible.

Victor runs to the mountains but the Creature locates him and tells him his story. When the Creature ran from Victor, he wandered into a shed attached to a cottage. In the cottage, the father taught an Arabian woman how to speak English. The Creature watched these lessons from a crack in the shed and taught himself how to speak and write. Eventually, the family discovered the Creature and they were horrified. Enraged, the Creature burned the cottage down.

The Creature tells Victor that if he creates a female for him, he will leave Victor alone. Victor agrees.

Victor travels to the Orkney Islands to devise the female but worries that the creatures will mate and form new abominations. Victor kills her, not knowing that the Creature is spying on him through a window. The Creature confronts Victor and vows to see him again at his wedding to his beloved, Elizabeth.

The Creature kills Victor's friend Henry. Since Victor was the last person seen with him, he is imprisoned for the murder. Eventually, he is acquitted so he returns home to Geneva.

After Victor marries Elizabeth, he asks her to wait in the bedroom as he looks for the Creature. However, the Creature finds a way into the room and kills Elizabeth. Victor enters as he sees the Creature fleeing with her corpse. The shock of Elizabeth's murder kills Victor's father. He literally follows the Creature to the ends of the Earth as Victor pursues him to the North Pole. He locates the Creature and chases him on his sled but he exhausts himself and passes out. This concludes Victor's story.

As the journey becomes more perilous, Captain Walton turns the ship around and prepares to return home. Victor dies shortly after.

Later, Walton finds the Creature on the ship grieving for his creator. The Creature feels more alone than ever now that his "father" is dead. He leaves and is never seen again.

29.
<u>Oliver Twist</u>
by Charles Dickens
1838

After being kicked out of his workhouse, a young orphan flees to London and tries to survive living on the streets.

Oliver Twist's mother dies in childbirth, leaving young Oliver to be sent to a farm to work. When he turns nine, Oliver is sent to a workhouse managed by Mr. Bumble. Oliver hates it there and is forced to eat gruel every day. One day, his friends decide to draw straws to see which one of them will go up to Bumble to ask for a second helping. Oliver draws the short straw and is forced to ask for more from Bumble. Bumble is outraged and casts Oliver out of the workhouse. Oliver is forced to work for an undertaker but he hates it there so much, he runs away to London, hoping his luck will change for the better.

But London is not as welcoming as he hoped. As he starves on the street, a teenage pickpocket sees young Oliver and takes an interest in him. This pickpocket is called Jack Dawkins but he likes to be known as The Artful Dodger. Dodger takes Oliver to an old crooked house where he meets the carer; a horribly disheveled, old man called Fagin. Fagin forces several orphans to pickpocket for him so he can live off the spoils in exchange for shelter. Fagin takes Oliver in.

Dodger steals a handkerchief from the bookkeeper, Mr. Brownlow. Brownlow realizes he has been robbed and chases the boys. The boys get away and Brownlow only finds Oliver, who is innocent of the crime. Mr. Brownlow can see that Oliver is too innocent to have committed the theft. Brownlow also notices that Oliver has a striking resemblance to a portrait of a woman in his house. Brownlow takes Oliver into his home and looks after him.

When Fagin realizes that Oliver has left, he worries that he will squeal to the cops about his pickpocketing scheme. He sends his monstrous henchman, Bill Sikes to track him down. Sikes' girlfriend, Nancy accompanies him. Sikes finds Oliver and brings him back to Fagin. Fagin needs Oliver because his small size will be advantageous for breaking into buildings. Oliver can stand on Sikes' shoulders and enter houses through their top windows, unlock the front door from the inside, allowing Sikes to enter and steal all he can carry. When Oliver breaks into a house, a servant shoots the boy and Sikes abandons him. The houseowners, Mrs. Maylie and her niece, Miss Rose, are concerned for the poor boy so they take Oliver in and look after him.

Nancy learns that Fagin and a man called Monks are desperate to recapture Oliver. It seems that Oliver was left a gold locket from his mother when she died. Monks obtains and destroys the locket. Nancy locates Mrs. Maylie and Mr Brownlow and warns them.

When Sikes learns of Nancy's betrayal, he corners her and beats her to death. Sikes runs away to hide by climbing up to a rooftop. As he climbs down a rope, he slips and the rope wraps around his neck, killing him.

Oliver goes back to Mr. Brownlow. When Brownlow learns of Fagin's and Monks' scheme, he confronts the pair.

It turns out that Monks is Oliver's half-brother. Oliver's father, Leeford was married to a rich woman but he was so unhappy with her that he had an affair with Agnes Fleming, Oliver's mother. Oliver was oblivious to this so Monks inherited Oliver's share of the wealth. Brownlow forces Monks to sign over Oliver's share.

Moreover, it is revealed that Rose is Agnes' sister which makes her Oliver's aunt. They adopt Oliver and live happily ever after.

30.
Nicholas Nickleby
by Charles Dickens
1839

Nicholas tries to survive in spite of experiencing hardships from all directions.

When Nicholas Nickleby's father dies, Nicholas and his family are forced to move to London and live with his cruel uncle, Ralph. Nicholas gets a job in a Yorkshire school as the assistant of the headmaster, Wackford Squeers. Nicholas attracts the attention of Squeers' daughter, Fanny. She falls for Nicholas but learns the feeling isn't mutual. She has his friend, Smike beaten to a pulp by Squeers. Outraged, Nicholas attacks Squeers and leaves the school. An acquaintance of Fanny called Browdie admires Nicholas for standing up to Squeers and helps him escape. Smike decides to leave the school with Nicholas and the two head to London.

Nicholas visits the employment office and sees a beautiful girl called Madeline.

While at a business party at Uncle Ralph's house, he uses the beauty of his sister, Kate to win favour with his guests, especially Lord Verisopht. Kate leaves after a guest called Mulberry Hawk, makes advances on her.

Nicholas enters Ralph's home just as his uncle reads a letter from Fanny explaining Nicholas' attack on Squeers. He tells Nicholas to leave London or Ralph will evict his family.

Hawk is outraged that Kate rejected him so he tracks her down. Ralph's clerk, Noggs learns of her mistreatment and writes to Nicholas. Nicholas returns to London.

Nicholas overhears Hawk and Verisopht in a coffeeshop mocking Kate. As they leave and make their way onto their carriage, Nicholas jumps on and demands to know Hawk's name. Hawk and Nicholas fight, which causes the carriage to crash. The crash enrages Hawk beyond control. Sadly, Hawk kills Verisopht in a frenzy.

Nicholas returns to the employment office and meets Charles Cheeryble; a rich merchant who runs a business with his brother, Ned. Charles hires Nicholas and provides a house for his family. Squeers makes his way to London and joins with Ralph to exact his vengeance on Nicholas. They run into Smike on the street and kidnap him. Browdie happens to be in London and learns of Squeers' plan. When he learns that Squeers has kidnapped Smike, Browdie rescues the boy. Smike tracks down Nicholas and tells him everything that's happened. Nicholas invites Browdie to dinner. Charles' clerk, Tim also attends the party.

Squeers presents a forged document to Tim stating that Smike is the son of Squeer's friend. Sadly, Smike is taken away by Squeers. He dies of tuberculosis soon after.

While at work, Nicholas encounters Madeline again. He learns that she is the daughter of Walter Bray who is heavily in debt.

A miser called Gride offers to pay the debt that Ralph is owed by Walter in exchange for his help. Gride has come into possession of the will of Madeline's grandfather, which leaves her a fortune if she marries. He and Ralph bully Walter to force his daughter to marry Gride. Walter is so ill, he can't put up a fight and so, accepts their terms. On the wedding day, Walter can't silence his guilt and he reveals the fact that Gride bullied him to have Madeline married. Walter dies and Madeline abandons the wedding.Noggs learns that Gride is in possession of the will and has him arrested. Ralph is confronted by the Cheeryble twins and told that Smike is dead. Ralph is overjoyed knowing that Smikes can't implicate him. But the twins inform him that Smike was Ralph's long-lost son. He believes that neglecting his son led to his death and so, Ralph commits suicide. Squeers' mistreatment of pupils in his school is uncovered and he's transported to Australia. Nicholas marries Madeline and they live happily ever after.

31.
<u>The Pit and the Pendulum</u>
by Edgar Allen Poe
1842

An imprisoned man finds himself strapped down as a swinging blade descends upon him.

During the Spanish Inquisition, a man is tried by several corrupt judges. As he awaits his verdict, he looks at seven long white candles on a table in front of him. He sees the candles melting as time goes by. He sees the candles representing his chances of being free as they melt away.

Sure enough, he is sentenced to death. It is unknown what crime he is accused of or if he has even committed the crime.

He is put into a pitch-black cell. To pass the time, he walks around the edges of the room and counts his paces to see how big the room is. He faints from exhaustion before he achieves this.

When he wakes up, he notices that there is food and water beside him.

He tries to measure the room again. The perimeter measures a hundred steps. As he walks through the room, he trips on his robe. As he slips, he realizes that he nearly fell into a vast pit in the center of his cell.

The man faints again. When he awakens, he notices that there is a small light this time so he can see his surroundings. He discovers that he is tied down to a flat wooden board by ropes.

He looks upward at the ceiling to see a painting of Father Time. Hanging from the ceiling is an enormous pendulum with a 1ft long crescent scimitar blade at the bottom. The blade is razor sharp and the pendulum is swinging from side to side, gradually making its way downward. As it descends, the man realizes that it will eventually cut him in half.

He gets some meat from the food he was left earlier and uses it to get the attention of rats. The rats start to chew through the ropes.

When the pendulum is mere inches away from his chest, he breaks free. The pendulum reverses itself and heads back up to the ceiling.

He notices that the walls have become boiling hot and have begun to close inwards. The man realizes that he will eventually be forced into the hole in the centre or he will be crushed to death.

With only seconds left he prepares to jump into the pit as his only possible means of escape. Suddenly, he hears voices, a loud trumpet, and a gigantic explosion. He sees the walls reversing their direction.

A French general grabs the prisoner just before he falls into the pit. The French have taken over the Spanish region of Toledo. The man is saved.

32.
The Tell-Tale Heart
by Edgar Allen Poe
1843

A man gets away with murder but is driven mad with guilt as he can't stop hearing the dead man's deafening heartbeat.

This tale revolves around an unnamed narrator who is prone to nervousness and hyperactive sensitivity. His senses are so overly strong, he can't stand to look at the old man he lives with because one of his eyes is too blue. He has no problem with the old man's personality; he just can't stand the eye. It drives him berserk, until he decides to kill the old man. As he plots the murder, he convinces himself that he is sane because an insane man would kill the old man on a whim but a sane man would plan it out.

Every night, the narrator opens the door for the old man in order to shine some light on the old man's "evil eye" to make himself erupt into a murderous frenzy. His plan doesn't work because the old man's evil eye is always closed.

On the eighth night, the narrator makes a noise in his sleep which awakens the old man. The narrator wakes up and lights his lantern. The light from his lantern is drawn directly to the evil eye of the old man. The narrator can hear the old man's heart pounding in terror. He sees this as the perfect moment to kill him. He smothers the old man in his bed.

The narrator chops up the body and hides it under the floorboards. He cleans up the room so there is no evidence of a murder.

But a neighbor reports to the police that he heard a scream on the night of the old man's murder.

Three police officers arrive and the narrator welcomes them in, believing that there is no possible way that they can find anything suspicious to arrest him for.

He tells the officers that the old man is away and will be back soon. When the police enquire about the screaming, the narrator explains that he is responsible for the screams after suffering a nightmare.

Out of arrogance, the narrator brings out chairs and lets the police sit directly above the floorboards where the old man is buried under.

At first, the narrator feels calm but suddenly hears a sharp ringing in his ears. The ringing becomes louder and louder until the narrator believes it must be the heartbeat from the old man.

Although the pounding sound gets louder, the police don't seem to react to it. In spite of the officers not hearing the heartbeat, the narrator becomes convinced that they are onto him.

The narrator breaks down and confesses to the crime. Bewildered by his sudden outburst, the police officers break open the floorboards to reveal the dead body. They arrest the narrator for the old man's murder.

33.
The Three Musketeers
by Alexandre Dumas
1844

Three has-been Musketeers join with a wannabe knight to stop an evil plot.

It's 1625 in France and the novel begins with a poor young nobleman called D'Artagnan leaving his family to become a Musketeer; a personal guard for the King and Queen.

He makes his way to Paris with a letter written to the commander of the Musketeers, Treville. While stopping at an inn, a man called Rochefort insults D'Artagnan. D'Artagnan challenges Rochefort to a duel. Rochefort's friend hits d'Artagnan with a cooking pot, rendering him unconscious. His letter is stolen by one of Rochefort's men and D'Artagnan vows vengeance.

D'Artagnan meets Treville at his headquarters, but without his letter, he cannot be considered as one of the king's personal guards. D'Artagnan sees the man who robbed him outside the window. He rushes outside and bumps into three Musketeers – Athos, Porthos, and Aramis. Outraged by D'Artagnan's rudeness, they challenge him to a duel.

That afternoon, D'Artagnan begins his first duel against Athos. An evil cardinal called Richelieu orders the Musketeers to be arrested for illegal dueling. Richelieu's guards attempt to capture the men but D'Artagnan and the Musketeers battle against them and emerge victorious. Richelieu is so impressed with his fighting prowess, D'Artagnan is rewarded with a small fortune and is made one of the King's guards.

With his newfound wealth, D'Artagnan finds lodgings and hires a servant called Planchet. One day, his landlord, Bonacieux visits D'Artagnan and implores him to save his wife, Constance. Constance is Queen Anne's confidante and Bonacieux worries she was kidnapped because she had knowledge of the queen's affair with the Duke of Buckingham. Her husband, King Louis XIII gives Anne a diamond stud as a gift and she passes it on to the Duke.

King Louis demands that his wife wears the diamonds for an upcoming party. However, Richelieu has sent an agent to Britain to take the diamonds from the Duke. Richelieu hopes this tension can instigate a war between England and France.

D'Artagnan decides to head to England so he can retrieve the diamonds before the agent steals them. He makes his way to England along with the Musketeers and Planchet. Unfortunately, the Cardinal's henchmen corner the Musketeers. Only D'Artagnan and Planchet reach London.

By the time D'Artagnan reaches the Duke, Richelieu's agent, Milady has already stolen the diamonds. Luckily, the Duke's jeweller can make exact copies of them and he gives them to D'Artagnan. He returns them to the queen in Paris. D'Artagnan is then sent to the siege of La Rochelle.

In an inn, the Musketeers hear Richelieu asking Milady to kill the Duke. The trio head to La Rochelle to warn the Duke. Milady is arrested but she seduces her guard and convinces him to let her out. She hides in a convent that Constance happens to be staying in. Milady poisons Constance in revenge against D'Artagnan. Before she has a chance to report back to Richelieu, she is arrested and executed.

The four men return to the siege where they are arrested and taken to Richelieu. The Cardinal says he is impressed by D'Artagnan's spirit and he is promoted to lieutenant.

The siege ends in 1628. Aramis retires to a monastery, Porthos gets married, and Athos serves as a Musketeer under D'Artagnan's tutelage until 1631.

34.
The Count of Monte Cristo
by Alexandre Dumas
1844

An innocent man is locked away for years and plots his revenge.

Edmond Dantes is a successful sailor from Marseille who is about to marry his fiancée, Mercedes, and be promoted to captain. But his colleague, Danglers is jealous of his promotion and his cousin, Fernand is in love with Mercedes. As a scheme to get Dantes out of the picture, they accuse him of being a traitor to his country. The prosecutor, Villefort, happens to be Dantes' neighbor. To avoid having any association with the accused, he sentences Dantes to life imprisonment without trial.

After six years in prison, Dantes considers suicide. A prisoner from the neighboring cell called Faria the Mad Priest tunnels his way into Dantes' cell assuming he is tunneling out of the prison. Over eight years, Faria educates Dantes and makes him understand that his incarceration wasn't an accident but a deliberate action by Fernand.

Faria realizes that he will die soon of old age. He tells Dantes of a treasure on the island of Monte Cristo. Faria perishes soon after.

When a prisoner dies, the guards take the corpse away in a sack. Dantes moves Faria into his own cell and he puts himself in the sack. The guards throw the sack into the sea and Dantes swims to an island where he is rescued by smugglers.

He works for the smugglers for several months, until one day their ship passes Monte Cristo. Dantes fakes an injury to make them stop the ship and leave him on the island to recover. As they leave, he locates the treasure. With his newfound wealth, he buys a yacht and returns to Marseille. He buys the title of Count and the island of Monte Cristo itself. Dantes learns that all of his friends and family have died or live in poverty. All of his enemies have become wealthy and successful.

While Dantes visits Rome, he meets Albert, who is the son of his former fiancée and Fernand, who is now the Count de Morcerf. He has Albert kidnapped by a friend so he can "rescue him" as an excuse to meet his mortal enemy, Fernand. It's been so long that Fernand doesn't recognize Dantes. Dantes gains a great reputation because of this rescue and easily enters Fernand's social circles.

Mercedes is the only person to recognize Dantes. Dantes uses his wealth, status, and cunning to destroy the fortunes and reputations of Fernand and all of his friends.

Dantes makes it public knowledge that Fernand has had innocent people enslaved in the past. Fernand is put on trial and socially shamed.

When Fernand's son, Albert learns that it was Dantes who tarnished his father's name, he challenges him to a duel. Mercedes tells Albert who Dantes is and how Fernand ruined his life. Now knowing the truth, Albert and Mercedes ostracise Fernand. Fernand learns of Dantes' identity and commits suicide.

Mercedes and Albert leave to make a new life for themselves. Sadly, Dantes' revenge doesn't stop there. He destroys the life of Villefort, the prosecutor who condemned him to prison. He manipulates Villefort's wife and son into committing suicide. When Villefort discovers this, Dantes reveals who he is. This revelation leaves Villefort utterly deranged.

Dantes worries that he has gone too far but when he revisits his old prison, he realizes that his revenge is just. Dantes uses his vast wealth to manipulate the bond market (the old fashioned version of the Wall Street Stock Market), which leaves his other enemy, Danglers, bankrupt and mad. With his enemies vanquished, he leaves to begin a new life.

35.
The Snow Queen
by Hans Christian Anderson
1844

A boy is manipulated by an ancient evil, which allows a powerful witch called The Snow Queen to claim him as her slave.

An evil troll makes a magical mirror that will only reflect the ugly side of whoever looks into it. He teaches other trolls how to use the mirror. They travel the world with the mirror, distorting everything they see.

The trolls attempt to fly to Heaven to make God himself look foolish in the mirror. The closer they get to heaven, the more the mirror shakes with excitement. The mirror shakes so hard, the trolls lose their grip and it falls back to earth, shattering into a million pieces.

All of these tiny pieces find their way into the hearts of humanity. As a result, humanity becomes insecure and cynical, not only about themselves but about other people.

Years pass, and the story focuses on a boy called Kai and his neighbor, Gerda. Gerda loves the flowers that bloom in the summer because they remind her of how much she loves Kai.

One night, Kai looks out his window and sees a woman. Kai recognizes her as The Snow Queen from his grandmother's stories. She is a magical being that can control bees made of snow. She urges him to follow her, but Kai is too scared to leave his room.

One summer, a piece of glass from the evil mirror gets blown into Kai's eyes and heart. He becomes corrupted by the mirror shards and starts acting nastily to Gerda and his grandmother. The only things he loves now are snowflakes.

That winter, he plays in the snow and eventually encounters The Snow Queen. She kisses him twice. Each kiss creates a magical spell; the first kiss makes him immune to the cold and the second kiss makes him forget about his family and Gerda.

The Snow Queen takes Kai to her palace in her sleigh. With Kai missing, people assume he has drowned in a river. Gerda offers the river her shoes if it returns Kai. The river tells Gerda that it cannot give Kai to Gerda because he didn't drown there.

Gerda visits an old witch for help. The nasty witch conjures a spell that makes Gerda forget about Kai. The witch buries her flowers in the earth, knowing that they will make Gerda remember him. Gerda's tears uplift a bush, which tells Gerda that while it was buried into the earth it could feel everyone that was dead and Kai was not one of them.

Gerda runs away and meets a crow that tells her that Kai may be at the princess' palace. Gerda makes her way there and meets the prince and princess. She tells them of her quest for Kai. They offer her a coach and while she travels in it, robbers bring her to their hideout.

She befriends a girl there who has a pet dove. The dove tells Gerda that The Snow Queen took Kai to Lapland. A reindeer called Bae tells Gerda he knows how to get to Lapland so the two of them make their way to find Kai.

They reach The Snow Queen's palace. As Gerda enters, she finds Kai trapped by the queen's magic in a frozen lake.

Gerda kisses him and her love releases him from The Snow Queen's spell. The kiss also destroys the corruption in his heart from the broken piece of mirror. They leave the palace and return home.

36.
__Wuthering Heights__
by Emily Bronte
1847

An estate owner adopts a poor boy who falls for his foster sister.

Lockwood, who rents Thrushcross Grange, meets his landlord, Heathcliff, who lives in Wuthering Heights. A storm forces Lockwood to stay the night in Heathcliff's home. In his bedroom, he sees books owned by Catherine, who used to live there. At night, Lockwood has a nightmare that Catherine is climbing through the window. His screams awaken Heathcliff who bursts in. Lockwood explains what he saw which deeply disturbs Heathcliff.

The next day, Lockwood returns to the Grange. Lockwood asks the servant, Nelly about Wuthering Heights. She tells him that 30 years ago, Earnshaw lived there with his children, Hindley and Catherine. On a trip, Earnshaw saw a "dark-skinned gypsy boy." He adopted him and called him Heathcliff. Catherine and Heathcliff became close but Hindley was jealous of him. When Earnshaw died, Hindley inherited Wuthering Heights.

A few months later, Heathcliff and Catherine spied on the Lintons who live in the Grange. Catherine is caught and attacked by a dog. The Lintons care for Catherine as she heals. Heathcliff is sent back to Wuthering Heights. The Lintons were posh and their manners and habits rub onto Catherine. When she returns to Wuthering Heights, she acts more aristocratic and snobbish. She starts to look down on Heathcliff.

As the Lintons visit the next day, Heathcliff dresses smartly to impress Catherine but he ends up arguing with Edgar Linton. Hindley chucks Heathcliff into the attic.

Later, Hindley's wife, Frances, gives birth to Hareton and she dies shortly after.

As the years pass, Catherine falls in love with Edgar. Heathcliff overhears her tell Nelly that she doesn't love Edgar as much as Heathcliff. When he hears Catherine say it would be degrading to be married to Heathcliff, he runs away.

Edgar and Catherine get married. Six months later, Heathcliff returns as a successful gentleman. Edgar's sister, Isabella falls for him. Heathcliff hates her but embraces her to spite Catherine. One day, Edgar catches Heathcliff and Isabella being affectionate, which causes an argument. Distraught, Catherine locks herself in a room and makes herself ill.

Heathcliff lives at Wuthering Heights and gambles with Hindley until Hindley loses everything to Heathcliff. Heathcliff elopes with Isabella. When he returns, he visits Catherine who is still ill. He also learns that she is pregnant. She gives birth to Cathy the next day and dies. Isabella leaves Heathcliff and gives birth to Linton. Hindley dies soon after, leaving Heathcliff in charge of Wuthering Heights. 12 years later, Edgar discovers that Isabella is dying and leaves to adopt her son, Linton. When he returns with his son, Heathcliff insists that Linton should live with him, hoping Linton will marry Cathy who is now a teenager.

A year later, Edgar becomes ill. Heathcliff says Cathy can see her father if she marries Linton. Linton takes no part in this manipulation and allows Cathy to leave to see her father before he dies. Linton dies shortly after. Hindley's son Hareton is kind to her but she withdraws from the world. This ends Nelly's story. Lockwood leaves soon after.

Months later, Lockwood returns to the Grange. He sees Nelly and asks how things are. She tells him how Hareton had a farm accident and became close to Cathy as he recuperated. They are now engaged. During this time, Heathcliff stopped eating. He would wander the moors desperately trying to find Catherine's ghost. Four days later, he was found dead in Catherine's old room. He was buried beside her. The story ends with Lockwood passing the graves of Edgar, Catherine, and Heathcliff.

37.
Jane Eyre
by Charlotte Bronte
1847

A timid girl softens the heart of her employer until she learns of his dark secret.

Jane Eyre lives with her nasty aunt, Sarah Reed, who mistreats and neglects her. She's eventually sent away to school (much to her aunt's delight) where she continues to be mistreated. Because the school is cold and unclean, many students become ill and die.

Six years later, Jane becomes a teacher herself. Two years after that, she leaves the school. She advertises her services and a woman called Alice Fairfax replies. Alice is the housekeeper at Thornfield Hall. Jane accepts the job and teaches a French girl called Adele Varens how to speak English.

Whilst out walking one night, a horseman rides by Jane and the horse slips on ice, hurling the horseman to the ground. Jane helps him back on the horse. Later, she discovers the man is the master of Thornfield Hall, Edward Rochester, and they become close friends.

One day, a fire erupts in Rochester's room. Jane puts it out and rescues him.

Jane receives a letter from her aunt, Sarah, asking for her. Sarah had a stroke after her son died. Jane returns to look after her. Before Sarah passes away, she tells Jane that she was wrong about her. Sarah tells her that Jane's uncle, John, wanted Jane to live with him but Sarah told him that she passed away. Sarah dies soon after.

Jane returns to Thornfield as Rochester prepares for his marriage to a horrible woman called Blanche Ingram. Rochester says he will miss Jane when he is married. Jane confesses that she has feelings for him. Rochester decides to marry her instead of Blanche.

Jane writes to her Uncle John, telling him that she's engaged. Before her wedding, a woman sneaks in and tears Jane's veil. Rochester believes it is a servant called Grace.

At the wedding ceremony, Rochester's guest, Mason makes an announcement. He reveals that Rochester is already married to Mason's sister, Bertha.

Rochester says he was forced into that marriage by his father to get her money. Once they were married, Rochester realized Bertha was insane and she was locked away in the attic. Grace the servant was hired to attend her. One day, Bertha escaped and she was responsible for starting the fire and tearing the veil.

Jane is very upset and humiliated, so she runs away. She eventually finds herself without food or money. Out of exhaustion, she faints near a house owned by The Rivers' family - Diana, Mary, and St John. The Rivers' family nurses her back to health. When she feels better, St. John finds a teaching job for her at a nearby school.

The sisters leave to pursue jobs, but St. John stays and becomes close with Jane. Jane tells him who she really is. St. John tells her that her uncle John has died, and he left her his entire fortune of £20,000 (over a £1 million by today's standards.)

It turns out that St. John knows this because John is HIS uncle too which makes him and Jane cousins!

Jane is overjoyed now that she has a family to call her own. Jane shares the money with the Rivers' family but has an impulse to find Mr. Rochester. She returns to his house to discover that it is in ruins. It turns out that his wife burned his house down before taking her own life. In a rescue attempt, Rochester lost his eyesight and hand. She decides to stay with him. They get married and he regains his sight just in time to see his first-born child.

38.
David Copperfield
by Charles Dickens
1849

After his parents' death, David's evil stepfather sends him to London where his life changes forever.

The story begins with an English boy called David Copperfield losing his father. David is cared for by his gentle housekeeper, Peggotty and his kind but frail mother, Clara.

When David is seven, his mother marries Edward Murdstone. Edward and his sister, Jane move into the house and David instantly takes a dislike to them.

One day, Edward tries to hit David for doing badly in school. David retaliates by biting him. As punishment, he is sent to boarding school. Before he attends school, Peggotty takes him to visit her family in Yarmouth. David meets Peggotty's brother, Mr. Peggotty and his two adopted children, Ham and Little Emily. They share with the widow of Mr. Peggotty's brother, Mrs. Gummidge.

David then starts school at Salem House, which is ruled by the evil Mr. Creakle. David becomes friends with two boys called James Steerforth and Tommy Traddles.

When David returns home for the holidays, he discovers that his mother has had a baby boy. Sadly, his mother and the baby died.

Edward makes David work for his business partner, Mr. Micawber in London. Micawber is awful at managing money so David flees to avoid building up debts.

He walks all the way to Dover where he finds his last living relative, his father's sister, Betsey. She agrees to look after him, even after Edward attempts to reclaim custody over David. Because of her eccentric ways, she renames him Trotwood Copperfield. She even nicknames him Trot.

Betsey sends David to a school run by Doctor Strong. David moves in with Mr. Wickfield and his daughter, Agnes who he becomes close friends with.

As David becomes a young man, he encounters Peggotty the housekeeper again. Peggoty has married a man called Mr. Barkis. She has also adopted her niece, Emily, who was an orphan. They move in with David who becomes very attached to Emily. However, David's schoolfriend, James, also becomes fond of her.

Betsey convinces David to become a lawyer. He becomes an apprentice at Spenlow and Jorkins' firm in London and he lodges with Mrs. Crupp. He meets Mr. Spenlow's daughter, Dora and falls in love with her.

David learns that Barkis is very ill and so, heads back home. Emily is devastated when Barkis dies. She believes she can only be happy again if she marries James. The two of them run away together which upsets Mr. Peggoty.

David fantasises about having a life with Dora but her father forbids it. Tragically, Dora's father dies in a carriage accident soon after. Without her disapproving father around, Dora marries David.

David learns that James has left Emily. Emily's heart is broken and she runs away. David and Mr. Peggoty search for Emily. When they find her, Emily and Mr. Peggoty decide to move to Australia.

Sadly, Dora dies shortly after having a miscarriage. David travels abroad to get his mind past this personal tragedy. As time goes by, he realizes that he is in love with Agnes Wickfield. When he meets her, he confesses his love. It turns out that she has always loved him. They get married and have children.

39.
The Scarlet Letter
by Nathaniel Hawthorne
1850

A Puritn town obsesses about a woman's affair.

This story takes place in 1642 during Puritan times in Boston. Hester Prynn falls pregnant but her husband has been lost at sea for two years. She is found guilty of adultery and is forced to forever wear a large scarlet "A" (which stands for adultery) on her dress as a public humiliation. The women demand to know who the father is, but she does not answer.

Hester sees a man in the crowd whom she recognises as her long-lost husband who is presumed dead. He happens to have returned to the town on the day of Hester's public humiliation by chance. When he learns of her adultery, he insists that the man she was with should be punished too.

Reverend Wilson and Minister Dimmesdale interrogate Hester about the man she slept with, but she refuses to name him.

She is brought to her cell and the guard brings in a physician to look after her. The physician happens to be her husband, who now goes by the name of Roger Chillingworth. He asks her who is the man she slept with. When she doesn't reveal his identity, Chillingworth insists that he will find out eventually. Chillingworth tells her not to reveal that he is her husband, or he will kill the man she had an affair with.

She is eventually released from prison and she finds a cottage on the edge of town to live in, so the locals won't bother her. She takes up needlework and makes very little money. She gives birth to a daughter whom she names Pearl. As her daughter grows up, Pearl becomes fascinated by the scarlet "A" on her mother's dress.

As Pearl grows older, she becomes bratty and hard to control. Because of Hester's stigma, rumors about Pearl start circulating and the church considers removing her from her mother. Afraid that she will lose her daughter, Hester speaks to Governor Bellingham as well as Reverend Wilson and Minister Dimmesdale. Dimmesdale convinces the governor to allow Hester to keep her child.

Dimmesdale's health begins to wane and the people want Chillingworth to replace him. Chillingworth insists that Dimmesdale's deteriorating health is from an unconfessed guilt, heavily implying that he is Pearl's father.

One night, Chillingworth pulls Dimmesdale's vest upward while he sleeps and sees a symbol on his chest. It is not clear to the reader yet what the symbol is.

Dimmesdale decides to admit that he is Pearl's father. He prepares to make his confession in the same place Hester was humiliated by the townspeople when they learned of the affair. Before he has a chance to confess to his crime in front of the townspeople, a meteor in the sky appears and forms a huge "A." As this happens, Pearl points to Chillingworth.

Days later, Hester tells Dimmesdale that her husband is Chillingworth. She removes her scarlet letter and demands that they start a life together in Europe. Pearl refuses to go with them unless Hester wears her scarlet letter.

Shortly after, Dimmesdale delivers the greatest sermon of his life. Afterward, he decides to confess to his affair with Hester. He reveals the scarlet "A" on his chest to the townspeople. Cleared of his guilt, he dies peacefully in Hester's arms. Chillingworth loses his desire for revenge and dies shortly afterwards.

Hester returns to her cottage and decides to wear the scarlet letter on her dress. When she dies, she is buried beside Dimmesdale. They share a single tombstone with a scarlet "A."

40.
<u>Moby Dick</u>
by Herman Melville
1851

A mad captain seeks revenge against a monstrous whale.

Ishmael travels from Manhattan to New Bedford and is preparing to sail on a ship. He stays at a crowded inn where he is forced to share a bed with a harpooner called Queequeg. Queequeg is a heavily tattooed Polynesian from a cannibalistic tribe.

The next morning, Ishmael and Queequeg sign up for a voyage on a whaler ship called the Pequod which is led by the mysterious Captain Ahab.

After the ship begins to set sail, Ahab reveals himself. He has a peg leg because he lost his leg when a white sperm whale called Moby Dick attacked his ship. The whale killed his entire crew, save for himself and he intends to use the Pequod crew to slay Moby to exact his revenge. The men are outraged that they were misled, believing that they were hired for a job, not a personal vendetta against a whale.

Each time the Pequod passes another ship, Ahab asks desperately if they have seen a white whale.

Queequeg develops a sudden fever that seems fatal. A carpenter forges a coffin for Queequeg but he makes a miraculous recovery shortly afterwards.

As the Pequod enters the Pacific Ocean, Ahab smells the same waters that Moby Dick swam in the last time he encountered the great beast. Ahab prepares a barbed harpoon covered in the blood of his men.

Impatiently waiting to confront the murderous whale, Ahab becomes prone to scolding his crew. As he approaches the Equator, a typhoon attacks the ship. Lightning strikes the mast. Ahab sees the lightning as a sign that Moby is near. The crew begins to worry for Ahab's sanity. A crewmember called Starbuck strongly considers shooting Ahab in his sleep.

The following morning, Ahab learns that the compass has been damaged by the storm. The ship heads southeast until they hear Moby Dick blow his spout. Ahab recognizes the sound because it sounds like a wild roar. They pursue Moby Dick but eventually lose track of him. Later, they encounter another ship called the Rachel that has lost five men to Moby Dick.

Ahab privately speaks to Starbuck about his own family. He regrets spending 40 years on the sea when he should've looked after his wife and child. Starbuck encourages his captain to return home but Ahab believes that he has come too far to give up now.

Not too long after, Ahab himself finally spots Moby Dick. Ahab hoists himself down onto a small boat with other crewmembers. With little warning, Moby bites Ahab's boat in two, dispersing the crew.

They chase the whale for a whole day. Ahab sends more boats and nets to ensnare Moby. Although they successfully lay a net on the whale, this attempt ends in failure with Ahab losing his ivory leg and a crewmember.

On the third day of the chase, Ahab lowers himself into a boat to attack Moby Dick. The whale destroys the ship and all of the boats. Ahab gets entangled in the net that he laid upon Moby Dick the previous day. Ahab thrusts his harpoon into the whale screaming, "From Hell's heart, I stab at thee!" The whale swims away carrying the mad captain to his death.

All of the crew die apart from Ishmael who only survives by hanging onto Queequeg's sturdy coffin. The Rachel ship passes through still looking for lost crew. They see Ishamel and rescue him.

41.
A Tale of Two Cities
by Charles Dickens
1859

An ex-aristocrat and a lawyer fall for a woman during the French Revolution.

The novel begins in 1775 with a bank worker called Jarvis Lorry who works in London. He meets Lucie and tells her that her supposed dead father is alive and imprisoned in France.

Lorry and Lucie make their way to a wine shop in Paris run by the Defarges, Ernest and Therese who are speaking to several Revolutionaries. Ernest takes Lucie to see her father upstairs. She sees that her father, Dr. Manette is making shoes. This is a skill he picked up whilst imprisoned in the Bastille prison, but it has now become an insane obsession. He only refers to himself as 105 North Tower which was the cell he was in. They take Manette back to England.

Five years later, Lucie's lover, Charles Darnay is put on trial for treason. Two spies called Barsad and Cly have revealed sensitive information to the French. To avoid being caught, they have framed Darney and testified against him. One witness claims he recognizes Darnay as a spy. Darnay's attorney, Stryver asks a lawyer called Sydney Carton to stand up. People are astonished at how similar he looks to Darnay. If they can mistake Carton for Darnay then surely the witness may have made a similar mistake. The witnesses' claim is made redundant and Darnay is acquitted.

18 months later, Darnay confesses to Manette that he loves his daughter. He is about to tell him of his family history but Manette stops him. Carton confronts Lucie and tells her he feels worthless but she inspired him to become a better person so he could deserve her.

Shortly after, Darnay and Lucie get married. Lorry notices that Manette seems rattled at the wedding. It is because Darnay told him that he is actually a nephew of the French tyrant, Marquis St. Evremonde. Evremondre was murdered which means that Darnay has inherited his title. This puts Darnay on top of the Revoluntionaries kill list.

The French Revolution begins a few years later. The Revolutionaries (led by the Defarges) storm the Bastille; a jail that represents tyranny. Ernest makes his way to Manette's cell in 105 North Tower. They find something important, but it is not clear what until later.

Lorry's bank sends him to France to make sure the French branch is stable. Darney heads to France to resolve his inheritance. He is arrested as soon as he arrives. Manette and Lucie make their way to France and beg the Defarges to free Darnay but they refuse.

A year later, Darnay's trial begins. Darnay claims that he renounced his family name because he was ashamed that they gained their wealth by oppressing the poor. Manette defends him. The people sympathise with Manette as being a prisoner of the Revolution and so, Darnay is proven innocent. He leaves but is arrested again on new charges but Darnay doesn't know who the accuser is.

At Darnay's new trial, his accusers are announced – Ernest, Therese and… Manette! The mysterious item that Ernest found in Manette's cell was a letter he wrote that condemned the Evremondre family. Since Evremondre is dead, Darnay has inherited the title of Marquis and he must be sentenced to die for his family's sins.

Carton goes to Darnay's cell as he prepares for his execution. Carton drugs Darnay and switches clothes with him so he can die in his place. Carton does this so Lucie can be with the one she loves. Darnay is brought to the Manettes and they leave Paris.

Carton is guillotined along with 51 other people. No man had ever been more at peace before facing the guillotine.

42.
Great Expectations
by Charles Dickens
1861

A mysterious benefactor remodels a humble orphan into a gentleman.

It's Christmas Eve, 1812 and a seven-year-old orphan called Pip visits his family graves. Suddenly, he bumps into an escaped convict. The convict demands that Pip steal food for him. Pip reluctantly obliges until the police arrest the convict the next day.

Pip lives with his horrible older sister, Mrs. Joe and her kind husband, Joe the blacksmith. A woman called Miss Havisham contacts Joe's uncle to find a boy to play with her adopted daughter, Estella. Havisham is a wealthy spinster who always wears a wedding dress. Pip routinely visits Havisham and Estella in her dark mansion, Satis House. Havisham urges Pip to love Estella. Pip falls for Estella even though she is cold to him and looks down on him for being lower class.

One day, someone gets into an argument with Mrs. Joe and leaves her brain-damaged. The suspect is an escaped prisoner, which makes Pip feel guilty that it is the convict he fed.

A lawyer called Mr. Jaggers informs Pip that he is to inherit money from an unknown benefactor. Jaggers tells Pip that he must head to London to be taught how to be a gentleman. Pip believes that if he becomes a gentleman, Estella will love him. He assumes that Havisham is the benefactor.

Pip stays at a house with a relative of Havisham called Herbert Pocket. Pocket tells Pip how Havisham was jilted at the alter by a man of lower class and she never recovered from the heartbreak. He doesn't realize that Havisham has sworn vengeance on all men and she wants Estella to break Pip's heart.

Over the years, Pip is moulded into the gentleman he wishes to be. He returns to Satis House, hoping to see Estella. Pip assumes Estella will fall for him but he learns she is to marry a horrible oaf called Bentley Drummle.

One night, a man enters Pip's house. The mysterious figure turns out to be Pip's benefactor – the convict! His name is Abel Magwitch and he has become very wealthy over the years. He wanted to repay Pip for his kindness to him long ago. Pip intends to help Magwitch flee by boat so he can evade prison again.

One day, as Havisham is tending to her fireplace, her dress catches fire. Pip tries to save her but her burns are too extreme and she is left an invalid. Havisham admits she was wrong about manipulating Pip and Estella. Pip learns from Jagger's housekeeper and from Pocket that Estella is actually Magwitch's daughter.

Later, Pip is attacked by a former worker of Joe called Orlick. It was Orlick that attacked Pip's sister years ago, not Magwitch. Pocket rescues Pip from harm. Pip and Pocket try to help Magwitch escape, but the police capture him.

Pip visits a gravely ill Magwitch in jail. Pip tells him that Estella is alive. Magwitch believed her to be dead, so this news allows him to die happily. Pip falls ill and is then arrested for a debt he didn't pay while he lived in London.

Pip faints and when he awakens, he finds that Joe is nursing him and has paid his debt. Pip realizes that he has neglected Joe for years and he vows to repay him. He heads to Egypt with Pocket and becomes a clerk.

11 years later, Pip returns to Satis House and meets Estella who was abused by her now deceased husband. She asks Pip to forgive her because tragedy has finally opened her heart. He takes her hand and they walk away from the ruins of Satis House.

43.
Journey to the Centre of the Earth
by Jules Verne
1864

A professor discovers an ancient manuscript that reveals there is a secret passage that leads to the centre of the Earth.

The story takes place in Hamburg, Germany, and focuses on Professor Lidenbrock. The novel begins with Lidenbrock running home after purchasing an ancient Icelandic manuscript. Lidenbrock and his nephew, Axel read through the book and find an encrypted message that they can't decipher. After hours of failed attempts, Axel realizes that the code has to be read backwards. The code says that there is a secret passage in Iceland that leads to the centre of the Earth.

They venture to Iceland immediately. Axel is terrified and tries to convince Lidenbrock that journeying to the centre of the Earth is a suicide mission. They arrive in Reykjavik where they meet their guide, Hans. The three of them reach the supposed entrance to the centre of the Earth – a volcano base. The volcano has three craters. According to the coded message, the entrance is through the one crater that is touched by the shadow of a nearby mountain peak at noon during the last few days in June.

But Lidenbrock has a problem - the weather is too cloudy to cast a shadow. Lidenbrock becomes impatient as July approaches. With two days to spare, the sun comes out and the correct crater is revealed.

As soon as they descend into the Earth, Axel gets separated from Hans and Lidenbrock. He gets lost for miles but because of the incredible acoustics of the subterranean caverns, they can hear each other over vast distances. They eventually reunite.

As they continue their descent, they reach a gargantuan cavern. This area is lit by electrically charged gas at the celing and has an enormous ocean, a rocky coastline, trees, and huge mushrooms.

The three men build a raft out of the trees and sail through the ocean. In the water, the professor sees two prehistoric sea creatures fighting each other. The group approaches an island that has a vast geyser. Lidenbrock dubs it, "Axel Island."

A lightning storm forces the party to land on the coastline. On the island, they see a herd of mammoths, massive plants, and supersized insects.

As the group press through a forest, Lidenbrock sees a 12ft-tall prehistoric man. Lidenbrock and Axel start to discuss the possibility that there is an entire prehistoric human civilization living underground.

As the men continue their journey, they see a marked passageway. They can't enter it due to a recent cave-in.

Using gunpowder, they blast the rocks believing that the other side will help them reach the centre of the Earth. Instead, they find a seemingly bottomless pit.

The trio are swept away as the sea rushes into the pit. After hours of being caught in the waves, they eventually find themselves in a large volcanic chimney filling with water and magma. They are blasted out of a side-vent of the volcano.

When they regain consciousness, they learn that they have been ejected from a volcanic island in Italy called Stromboli. Lidenbrock returns to Hamburg and is considered one of the greatest scientists of all time. Hans returns to Iceland and Axel marries his lover, Grauben.

44.
<u>Our Mutual Friend</u>
by Charles Dickens
1865

A man is to inherit a vast estate but he suddenly dies, leaving everyone scrambling to take the estate for themselves.

A wealthy miser dies and his fortune goes to his estranged son, John Harmon. The solicitor of the will, Mortimer Lightwood states that John can only inherit the money under one condition – he marries a woman called Bella Wilfer, whom he has never met. John was abroad when his father died. As he heads back home to London to claim the money, he goes missing. A man called Gaffer Hexam (who makes his living by robbing corpses of their valuables) finds a body washed up in the Thames River. The body has papers confirming his identity as John. As his identity is validated, there is a mysterious man called Julius Hanford present.

With no heir, the miser's estate is donated to his only two acquaintances – Mr. and Mrs. Boffin. They embrace John's fiancée, Bella Wilfer, into their home and pamper her every need. Julius Hanford enters the household (but now he goes under the name of John Rokesmith.) He demands to be the Boffins' secretary without pay.

Boffin hires a one-legged man called Silas Wegg to read to him in the evenings. Over time, Wegg convinces Boffin that he should live in a bigger house and Wegg takes the estate as his own. Wegg wants the estate because he believes there is treasure buried in the yard.

Hexam is accused of murdering John by a man called Roger Rogue Riderhood and his river robbing community ostracizes him. Hexam has a son called Charles who dreams of being a schoolmaster. His sister, Lizzie encourages Charles to leave his father. Hexam is found drowned soon after.

Lizzie lodges with a dressmaker called Jenny Wren. A barrister called Eugene Wrayburn takes a shine to Lizzie but learns that Charley's headmaster, Bradley Headstone fancies her too. Lizzie is worried that the men might fight to the death over her so she leaves.

Bradstone asks Riderhood to help him track down Lizzie. While Bradston looks for her, he sees Eugene. Bradstone viciously beats him and leaves him for dead. Luckily, Lizzie finds Eugene in the river and nurtures him. They get married soon after.

Mr. Boffin embraces his newfound wealth and becomes a miser. He starts acting nastily to Rokesmith when he learns that he loves Bella. This encourages her to fall in love with Rokesmith and they soon marry.

To save his own skin, Bradstone accuses Riderhood of the beating of Eugene. When he learns that Eugene is still alive, he realizes that it's only a matter of time before he's taken to prison. Overcome with terror, he grabs Riderhood and jumps into a lake and the two men drown.

Meanwhile, Wegg finds a will in the yard that nullifies the first will.

It is unveiled that Rokesmith is actually John Harmon, live and well. While he was travelling back to claim his inheritance, a man stole his possessions. The thief was the body they found. John created his new identity to spy on Bella to see if she was worth marrying. Mr. Boffin reveals that he was pretending to be horrible to test Bella's character.

Wegg points out that Boffin is not entitled to the estate. However, Boffin alerts Wegg that there was a third will that was written just before the miser died that stated that Boffin inherits everything.

The Boffins make John and Bella their heirs so they will inevitably inherit the estate and Wegg is left with nothing.

45.
Crime and Punishment
by Fyodor Dostoevsky
1866

A man kills an old pawnbroker for the good of society but becomes haunted by her death.

Rodian Raskolnikov struggles to pay his rent in St. Petersburg. He plots to rob and kill a rich elderly pawnbroker called Alyona. Alyona is a horrid woman whom Rodian believes has no redeemable qualities. Because of her old age, Rodian believes she'lll be dead soon. Her murder seems logical and even necessary as killing her and taking her money will ensure Rodian will live. As he makes preparations, he befriends a drunk called Semyon.

After much thought, Rodian enters Alyona's household and kills her with an axe. Her half-sister, Lizaveta enters the room just as Rodian commits the murder. He has no choice but to kill her too. Rodian steals some of Alyona's belongings and money before he leaves.

The murder becomes a popular topic of gossip in the neighborhood. Rodian can't help but show his guilt and dread when it is mentioned.

One day, he sees a carriage has hit Semyon. Semyon dies from his injuries and Rodian gives Semyon's family the money he stole from Alyona. Semyon has a teenage daughter called Sonya who has become a prostitute to support the family. Rodian develops a relationship with her.

Rodian's mother and sister, Dounia arrive. Dounia was a governess to a wealthy family. The head of the family is Arkady. He loves Dounia but he is married so she left to avoid complicating the relationship. She met a middle-class man called Pyotr. Desperate for money, she marries hm. She has come to St. Petersburg to meet him. Rodian finds Pyotr two-faced and vile and wishes Dounia would leave him.

A detective called Porfiry sees how suspiciously and erratically Rodian acts and suspects he is Alyona's killer.

Arkady arrives in St. Petersburg to seek out Dounia. He informs her that his wife is dead, and Arkady proves he only loved her. Dounia assumes that Arkady is not telling her the whole story about his deceased wife so she turns him down.

Although Porfiry is certain that Rodian is the killer, his case falls apart when another man is accused of the murder and a confession is beaten out of him during an interrogation.

Even though Rodian appears to have gotten away with it, he is racked with guilt. He confesses his crime to Sonya. She tells him that he must go to the police. Unbeknownst to Rodian, Arkady happens to be staying in a room beside Sonya and overhears the conversation. Arkady confronts Rodian and tells him that he knows the truth. As Arkady speaks about his own life, Rodian believes Arkady is a murderer as well.

Later, Dounia accuses Arkady of being responsible for his wife's death, which he denies.

Porfiry alerts Rodian of his suspicions and urges him to confess to obtain a reduction in his prison sentence. Rodian finds the idea of confessing tempting since he believes that Arkady will expose him.

Arkady accepts that Dounia will never love him so he takes his own life. Rodian learns of Arkady's suicide as he approaches the police station and realizes that he can get away with murder. But he decides to confess to his crimes as he made a promise to Sonya. He is sentenced to eight years of penal servitude in Siberia where Sonya follows him.

Dounia marries Rodian's friend, Razumikhin. As time passes, Rodian's guilt subsides.

46.
Little Women
by Louisa May Alcott
1868

Four poverty-stricken sisters try to survive in post-Civil War America.

The March sisters – Amy, Beth, Jo, and Meg, sit in their living room worrying about their poverty-stricken lives. They consider buying themselves presents for Christmas to cheer themselves up but then conclude that they should buy presents for their mother, Marmee.

Marmee receives a letter from her husband, who is currently serving in the Civil War. The letter encourages the girls to stay positive during harsh times.

On Christmas day, the girls wake to find books under their pillows. Marmee tells her daughters that she should give their breakfasts to a local poor family called the Hummels. An old neighbor called Mr. Laurence hears of the girls' generosity and rewards them with a feast.

The following week, Meg and Jo are invited to a New Year's Party at the house of a wealthy friend of Meg called Sally. At the party, Jo meets Mr. Laurence's grandson, Laurie. At the end of the night, he takes the girls home.

Jo refuses to let Amy attend with her to the theatre. Amy gets back at her by burning Jo's manuscript. Jo retaliates by nearly letting Amy drown while she's ice-skating.

Meg attends a party for her friend, Annie Moffat. The girls at the party are under the impression that Meg is to marry Laurie for his wealth.

Later in the year, the Marches form the Pickwick Club, where they write a family newspaper. A few weeks later, Jo allows Laurie to become a member of their club. Joe gets one of her stories published.

Over time, the Marches become more content and they no longer stress about trivial things like money.

One day, the family receives a telegram stating that Mr. March is in hospital in Washington DC. As Marmee attends her husband, the girls neglect their housework and friends. Beth is the only one who visits her neighbours, the Hummels. Sadly, she contracts scarlet fever from the Hummel baby. By the time Marmee returns, Beth is on the verge of death. Amy neglects her, worried that she might catch the disease.

Laurie's teacher, Mr. Brooke falls for Meg and they become engaged.

The story jumps forward three years. Mr. March is home from the war and Laurie is about to finish school. Meg has just gotten married to Brooke and is preparing to move in with him. Meg has twins and names them Demi and Daisy.

Jo is under the impression that Beth loves Laurie. Jo moves to New York to help Beth seduce Laurie. It is here that Jo meets a German teacher called Professor Bhaer. He helps her with her writing, and she falls in love with him. When she returns home, Laurie proposes to her, but she rejects him because of Beth. Tragically, Beth dies soon afterwards.

Amy and Laurie meet in France and they develop a relationship. They get married and return home. They eventually have a daughter and they name her Beth.

Bhaer comes to the Marches household to find Jo. He proposes to her and they marry a year later.

Jo inherits her aunt's house and she turns it into a boarding school for boys. The story ends with the girls together, each of them grateful for having each other.

47.
War and Peace
by Leo Tolstoy
1869

The story revolves around five aristocratic families in Russia during the Napoleonic era.

The year is 1805. In St. Petersburg, there is a gathering of five aristocratic families. The company includes the awkward but likeable Pierre, a socially charismatic prince called Andrei, Vassily Kuragin, his son, Anatole, and his daughter, Helene. Andrei finds his pregnant wife boring and decides to fight in the Napoleonic War.

In Moscow, we are introduced to the Rostovs – Ilya and Natalya and their four adolescent children – Natasha, Nikolai, Petya, and Vera. Nikolai has just joined the army.

As the Russians and Austrians are resisting Napoleon's army, Andrei and Nikolai charge through. Andrei is wounded and presumed dead.

Although Pierre is the illegitimate son of the Count, he is made the heir of his father's fortune. He marries Helene Kuragin but learns that she has been unfaithful. He confronts the other man and challenges him to a duel, nearly killing him. He leaves Helene soon after.

Andrei returns home just as his wife gives birth to a baby boy. She dies in childbirth. Andrei's devout sister, Mary raises his son instead. Andrei tries to repair the government.

The Rostov's wealth is dwindling due to Nikolai's gambling debts. To avoid selling their family estate, Nikolai is told to marry a wealthy heiress even though he is in love with his cousin, Sonya.

Years later, Natasha attends a ball and falls for Andrei. His father, Bolkonsky insists that they wait a year before they get married. In the meantime, Andrei begins travelling.

Natasha finds herself becoming attracted to Helene's brother, Anatole. As they prepare to elope, Andrei returns home. He learns of Natasha's betrayal and dumps her. Pierre finds Natasha attractive and consoles her. She falls ill after attempting suicide.

In 1812, Napoleon invades Russia and Andrei returns to active duty. Pierre becomes overwhelmed by patriotism (or insanity) when he convinces himself that he should personally assassinate Napoleon. Napoleon's forces invade Andrei's home. Bolkonsky attempts to protect it and dies from a stroke. Mary escapes and finds Nikolai and the two run to safety. Over time, they start developing feelings for each other.

Helene requests an annulment from Pierre so she can marry a foreign prince. When Pierre learns of this, he goes mad and disappears in Moscow.

As the war reaches its breaking point, the Rostovs prepare to evacuate. They find Andrei who has suffered a severe grenade injury. As they rescue him, Petya decides to join the army. The French take control over Moscow. The French identify Pierre as he wanders the streets and have him arrested.

Mary visits the Rostovs to see how Andrei is. With Natasha and Mary spending time together, they grow to respect each other. Andrei forgives Natasha before he dies.

The Russians send troops to Moscow as the French have abandoned it after suffering a defeat. A fight breaks out between the French and the Russians. Pierre is rescued but Petya is killed. Out of exhaustion, Pierre becomes ill for three months. When he recovers, he admits his love for Natasha, and she feels the same.

Natasha and Pierre get married. Nikolai marries Mary.

48.
The Idiot
by Fyodor Dostoyevsky
1869

Upon Prince Mishkin's return to St. Petersburg from an asylum, a daughter of a wealthy family tries to seduce him.

Prince Lev Mishkin is a descendant of one of the oldest and most noble Russian families. The novel begins with him arriving in St. Petersburg. He has been in a clinic in Switzerland for the last four years for his epilepsy and his supposed mental instability.

Mishkin's only family in St. Petersburg is his distant relative, Madame Lizaveta. She's the wife of the heavily respected and wealthy General Yepanchin. They have three daughters – Alexandra, Adelaida, and Aglaya.

Yepanchin has an egotistical assistant called Ganya who is in love with Aglaya, even though he is engaged to the beautiful Nastassya. She was the mistress of an aristocrat called Totsky and he has promised to pay Ganya a fortune if he breaks up with her.

Ganya knows that Mishkin is a buffoon so he openly talks about this dilemma with him present. The situation is complicated further when Ganya learns that a man called Rogozhin pursues Natassya. Ganya asks Mishkin if he believes that Rogozhin intends to marry her. Mishkin isn't mentally stable so he inappropriately replies that Rogozhin might marry Natassya but then kill her after a week.

Mishkin rents a room with Ganya and his family. Natassya enters and mocks Ganya's family for not accepting her as a potential wife. Rogozhin enters and offers Natassya a vast fortune. Natassya says she is having a party that night for her birthday where she will announce which man she will marry.

The party guests include Totksy, Ganya, Yepanchin, and many others. Mishkin arrives uninvited. As Natassya appears to choose Rogozhin, Mishkin offers to marry her, claiming that he has inherited a large sum of money. Despite his offer, Natassya leaves with Rogozhin.

Months pass and Natassya worries that she should've chosen Mishkin. Mishkin's fortune quickly dwindles due to debts and alleged relatives demanding payments.

Eventually, he visits Natyssa's house and is horrified when he learns that Rogozhin beats her. He attempts to kill Mishkin but Rogozhin freaks out when Mishkin starts to have an epileptic fit.

Mishkin moves to a nearby town. While there, he meets a man called Burdovsky. He claims that his father was the one who bequeathed the inheritance to Mishkin. It is clear the man is lying and is taking advantage of Mishkin's wealth. Nevertheless, the idiot prince obliges.

Mishkin spends most of his time with his family. He falls for Aglaya and, although she cares for him, she's too much of a snob to admit it publicly. However, her family seems to be under the impression that the two are engaged. Aglaya's family have a party to celebrate the couple. Mishkin suddenly has another fit. The family then decides that he's not suitable for Aglaya but Aglaya doesn't turn against him. Natassya has been writing to her, asking for Mishkin's hand in marriage. The two women confront Mishkin and force him to choose one as his wife. The simple prince can't make a decision, so the two women storm out.

Mishkin eventually heads to Natyssa's home and learns that Rogozhin has killed her in a rage. Rogozhin goes to jail and Mishkin becomes so unstable, he needs to check back into the mental health clinic.

49.
Twenty Thousand Leagues Under the Sea
by Jules Verne
1870

A sea explorer discovers a sea monster that may not be what it seems.

The story begins when several ships spot a gigantic sea monster. The American government assembles a team in New York to destroy the creature.

A marine biologist called Professor Pierre Aronnax receives an invitation to join the expedition, which he happily accepts. His servant, Conseil, and expert harpoonist, Ned Land joins him.

After a long journey at sea, they finally locate the monster. They attack the beast but their ship becomes heavily damaged in the battle. Pierre, Ned, and Conseil are thrown off the ship and land on the creature. They are surprised to learn that the creatur's exterior is metallic. The "sea monster" is actually a highly advanced submarine. The submarine's crew rescue the three men and they are led to the commander, the mysterious and reclusive Captain Nemo.

Nemo built the Nautilus submarine so that he could roam free throughout the ocean without having to deal with the rules of man on land. He tells Aronnax that his electrically powered ship is the most advanced vessel in the world.

Nemo is obsessed with discovery and knowledge but his self-made exile on the sea has made him go mad and he vows to have his vengeance against humanity.

Nemo enjoys the company of his guests, but he must keep them prisoner to ensure the existence of his ship is kept secret. Aronnax is fascinated by everything Nemo says. Ned on the other hand, makes plans to escape.

Aronnax and his men see the corals of the Red Sea, wrecked battleships at the bottom of the ocean, the ice of Antarctica, and the lost city of Atlantis.

Nemo lets Aronnax, Ned, and Conseil swim in the ocean in diving suits so they can hunt sharks with air guns.

The men have a funeral underwater for one of the original crew who died under suspicious circumstances.

As they continue their journey, they are attacked by octopi (it's usually mistranslated as Giant Squids) and one of the crew is killed.

Throughout the book, Nemo implies that he exiled himself when his family was killed in his home country, but he never elaborates.

At the end of the novel, the Nautilus is attacked by a warship from Nemo's unspecified country of origin. Nemo rams the ship in spite of Aronnax's pleas not to. Nemo smashes the other ship until it sinks to the bottom of the ocean.

Nemo gazes at a picture of his deceased wife and children and sinks into a depression. Overwhelmed by sadness, he neglects his duties as commander, allowing his ship to get sucked into a massive whirlpool.

Aronnax, Ned, and Conseil escape before the ship gets too near the whirlpool. They swim to a nearby island.

50.
Around the World in Eighty Days
by Jules Verne
1873

A man is challenged that he can't travel the world in eighty days.

The story revolves around an eccentric, rich Englishman called Phileas Fogg. While he is in a private members club, he reads in the newspaper that a new railway station in India will allow a person to travel the world in eighty days. The rest of the club members dismiss this notion, but Phileas is adamant it can be done. The club members bet him £20,000 (£1.6 million by today's standards.) He accepts the wager.

He and his French valet, Jean Passepartout, leave London by train at 845pm on Wednesday, October 2nd 1872. He must return before Saturday, Decemer 21st to win the bet.

As Phileas and Passepartout reach Egypt, a detective called Fix is pursuing a bank robber from London. He believes that Phileas is the criminal and so, boards the same steamer as him. He can't arrest the men without a warrant unless they are on British soil. They dock two days early in Bombay and they take a train to Calcutta. Phileas learns that the article he read about the Indian railway was incorrect. It doesn't go all the way to Calcutta. It stops in one location and starts again 50 miles away!

On their journey to the railway, they see an Indian woman called Aouda being prepared for a sacrifice and so, the men rescue her. They learn that Aouda has a distant relative living in Hong Kong. Phileas will be passing through Hong Kong on his journey, so he lets her join them until then. When they reach Hong Kong, Aouda learns that her relative has moved to Holland. Phileas decides to take her with him to Europe.

Since Hong Kong was part of the British Empire at the time, Fix can arrest Phileas. He confronts Passepartout and tells him that his friend is a criminal. Passepartout dismisses this accusation. To prevent him from warning Phileas, Fix drugs him. When he awakens, he assumes that Phileas has made his way onto the steamer to Yokohama. He dashes to the steamer and arrives just in time. But Philease didn't make it on time so Passepartout is travelling alone. When Phileas and Aouda arrive in Yokohama, they find Passepartout working at a circus. Reunited, the trio get on a steamer to San Francisco, unaware that Fix is still tracking them. The group travel to Yokohama and eventually make their way to New York. They encounter many problems; a falling bridge, bison crossing the track, the train being attacked by Native Americans, etc.

This delays the group so when they arrive in New York, they miss their ship to England. They find a steamboat heading to France. Phileas bribes the crew to take his party to England. The steamboat encounters a hurricane. Although nobody is harmed, it diverts the boats course and they run out of fuel. Phileas burns any wood they can find to keep it going.

The boat arrives in Ireland and it looks like they will have just enough time to reach London. But since Ireland was British soil at the time, Fix arrests Phileas. Luckily, they learn that the robber was caught in Edinburgh three days earlier and Phileas is freed.

The arrest delays Phileas so he arrives in London five minutes late. Philease apologises to Aouda because he was hoping he could look after her but now that he lost the bet, he will have to live in poverty. Aouda says she doesn't care because she loves Phileas and she wants to marry him anyway. Phileas prepares to pay the money but Passepartout points out that Phileas is wrong about the date. Since they travelled east, they gained an extra day. They arrive at the Reform Club victorious in the wager. Phileas marries Aouda and they live happily ever after.

51.
The Mysterious Island
by Jules Verne
1874

Five men land on an uncharted island that harbours many secrets.

The story begins during the American Civil War. As the death toll in Virginia escalates, five people escape death by hijacking a balloon.

The group is comprised of a railroad engineer called Cyrus, his black servant, Nebuchadnezzar, a sailor called Pencroff, his protégé named Herbert, and a journalist called Gideon.

After flying through a storm for several days, they crashland on an uncharted island in the South Pacific which they dub Lincoln Island.

Utilizing their skills, the five create fire, pottery, bricks, a ship, a house, and even a telegraph pole.

The five men start to notice strange occurrences on the island. One day, a box full of guns, tools, and ammunition suddenly appears with no explanation.

Shortly after that, the group finds a message in a bottle that tells them to rescue a castaway called Tom on a nearby island. They venture to the island and locate Tom but then get lost in a tempest on the way back. However, a mysterious fire beacon guides them back to Lincoln Island.

The five men learn that Tom was part of a crew of pirates and they have made their way to Lincoln Island to use it as their hideout. They fight with the five men until an unexplained explosion destroys the pirate ship, killing all but six pirates. The remaining pirates attack Herbert, severely injuring him.

The protagonists worry for their lives but suddenly find that the remaining pirates have perished mysteriously. There are no visible wounds on their bodies, so the five men are mystified by the cause of their death.

Herbert contracts malaria but is saved by the contents of a medical box that suddenly appeared in the men's house.

Not long after, the men learn the truth about the island. They find a port and a large submarine owned by an old bearded-man. The man is the commander of the Nautilus submarine, Captain Nemo. Nemo was assumed dead after his vessel was sucked into a whirlpool. It was he that provided the five men with the weapons and medicine they encountered. He was also responsible for destroying the pirate ship with a mine and he killed the pirates with an electric gun.

On his deathbed, Captain Nemo reveals that he is actually the Indian Prince, Dakkar. After the Indian Rebellion of 1857, Dakkar escaped to a deserted island with 20 of his men to build his Nautilus submarine. Upon its completion, he threw away his old identity and dubbed himself Captain Nemo (which is Latin for "Nobody.")

He warns the protagonists that a volcano is about to erupt, and it will destroy the island but they should be safe where they are.

Before he dies, Nemo cries out, "God and my country!" His body is put in the Nautilus, which serves as his tomb.

The volcano erupts, destroying the island but the men find themselves on the only piece above sealevel. Later, a rescue ship for Tom arrives and saves the five men.

52.
<u>The Adventures of Tom Sawyer</u>
by Mark Twain
1876

Tom and Huck's lives change forever when they witness a murder.

Tom Sawyer lives with his aunt, Polly, and his half-brother, Sid in a Mississippi town in Missouri. Tom gets into a fight and dirties his clothes. As punishment, he is forced to paint a fence. Tom tricks a kid to paint the fence for him by making it sound like an amazing experience. Tom makes the kid give him gifts in exchange for allowing him to paint the fence. Tom trades these gifts for Sunday School tickets. These tickets are given out to children who have memorized Bible verses and the superintendent is astonished by how many tickets Tom possesses. However, Tom's scheme is dashed when he is asked to name two of Jesus' disciples and his answer is David and Goliath.

Tom is in love with a new girl in town called Becky Thatcher. He convinces her to kiss him, which she sees as a sign of engagement. However, Becky learns that Tom has previously kissed a girl called Amy and so she assumes he is already engaged to her.

After she leaves him, Tom meets up with his friend, Huckleberry Finn, who is the son of the town drunk. They venture to the cemetery that night where they witness the murder of Dr. Robinson by a Native-American who is known as Injun Joe. They run away, swearing they will never tell a soul what they saw. However, Injun Joe's companion, Muff Potter, is accused of the crime, which makes the boys feel guilty.

Tom, Huck, and another friend called Harper run away to an island and pretend to be pirates to avoid encountering Injun Joe. Tom learns that the community believes the boys to be dead. He thinks it would be fascinating to attend his own funeral. Tom reveals himself to the townspeople and everyone is overjoyed to see him alive.

Later, a trial begins for Muff Potter. Racked with guilt, Tom testifies against Injun Joe claiming that he saw him kill Robinson. As a result, Muff is acquitted. Sadly, Injun Joe escapes before he gets convicted.

That summer, Tom and Huckleberry hunt for treasure in a house they believe is haunted. While they are looking upstairs, they hear something from below. Looking through a hole in the ground, they see Injun Joe hiding treasure. Each night, Huck returns, hoping to seize the treasure but he never has the chance.

Tom goes on a picnic to McDougal's Cave with Becky and their classmates. Tom wanders off with Becky until the two of them get lost. They find shelter in a cave.

That same night, Huck is at the haunted house and sees Injun Joe and an underling carrying a box outside. He follows them and hears their plan to attack a kind resident called Widow Douglas. Huck runs to fetch help, which makes the two robbers scarper. When Huck returns to the town, he learns that Tom is missing. The townspeople start searching for him.

Tom and Becky wander around the cave for a few days until they are weak and starving. Little do they know that Injun Joe uses the cave as a hideout. He suddenly appears to hide his treasure, but Tom and Becky get away and make their way back home.

The town judge decides to have the cave sealed off to prevent this ever happening again (not knowing that Injun Joe is inside.) When Tom hears of the sealing of the cave, he and Huck head to it and find Joe's corpse and the treasure. The two boys steal the treasure and head home. Widow Douglas decides to adopt Huck. Huck wants to run away from the community, but Tom tells Huck that he can be part of Tom's robber band if he stays with the Widow Douglas. Huck accepts Tom's proposal.

53.
Anna Karenina
by Leo Tolstoy
1877

A female aristocrat begins an affair that destroys her life.

An aristocrat from Moscow called Stiva has been caught cheating on his wife, Dolly. Stiva's sister, Anna Karenina is coming from St. Petersburg to encourage Dolly to stay with him.

Stiva's friend, Levin is coming to Moscow as well to propose to Dolly's sister, Kitty who is being pursued by an army officer called Count Vronksy.

At the train station, Anna sees Vronsky. Suddenly, a railway worker slips and falls in front of a train and dies.

Anna arrives at Stiva's house and convinces Dolly to forgive him.

Levin used to be promiscuous like Stiva, but he decides to leave that lifestyle and he wants to find his place in the world. Levin proposes to Kitty, but she rejects him as she prepares to seduce Vronsky at the upcoming debutante ball. However, Vronsky dances with Anna and they fall in love. When Anna returns to her husband Karenin, she realizes that she finds him unattractive.

Because of Anna's association with the Count, her status is elevated, and she becomes acquainted with more respected aristocrats including Vronksy's cousin, Princess Betsy. Betsy is glamorous and has many affairs. Anna loves this lifestyle, which makes it easy for Vronsky to seduce her. She gives in and they sleep together. Anna falls pregnant soon after.

Anna attends a horserace that Vronsky is racing in. Vronsky's horse collapses and Anna panics that he may be hurt. Karenin warns Anna that showing attention to another man is inappropriate. Anna confesses to him that she loves Vronksy. Karenin demands that she must end the affair, but she refuses. Karenin knows that a divorce will tarnish his reputation. He blackmails Anna to end the affair or he will take away her son, Seryozha.

After he learns that she nearly dies giving birth to Annie, Karenin forgives her. Anna and Vronksy run away together.

Stiva convinces Levin to meet Kitty again. They reconcile their differences and agree to marry. After they wed, Levin learns that his brother, Nikolai is dying from consumption. Kitty cares for Nikolai, making Levin realize that he is with the right woman. Kitty tells him that she's pregnant.

Anna and Vronsky start to resent each other. Anna has become ostracized because of her affair so Vronsky wants to socialize with his friends without her. They return to St. Petersburg and Anna tries to rejoin her old social circles but her former friends (including Princess Betsy) shun her. Vronsky and Anna leave for his old home. Anna believes that Vronsky will leave her, so she writes a letter to Karenin asking for a divorce.

They attend a club where they meet Levin and Stiva. Levin and Anna talk about their own personal problems. They put each other at ease. Levin tells Kitty he met Anna and she accuses him of being in love with her.

Kitty gives birth to Dmitri. Levin looks at his baby son and worries that he is not fit to be a father.

Stiva meets Karenin and asks him to grant Anna a divorce but he says no.

With Anna realizing she has no way out, she takes her own life by jumping in front of a train. During a thunderstorm, Levin fears for his wife's and son's lives. Because he is afraid for his family, Levin realizes that he does truly love them and accepts his role as a husband and parent.

54.
<u>Treasure Island</u>
by Robert Louis Stevenson
1883

Jim Hawkins comes into the possession of a treasure map, knowing that pirates are pursuing it.

Jim Hawkins is the son of an innkeeper who lives in Bristol, England. One day, a sea captain called Billy Bones bursts into the inn and pays Jim to be on the lookout for a one-legged man. Billy tells Jim that his crew is after him because they are seeking a sea chest that he is carrying. One day, a pirate enters and gives Billy a piece of paper with a Black Spot on it. The Black Spot represents a verdict from the pirates that the accused has been given six hours to live. Billy dies of a stroke almost instantly.

Jim takes Billy's sea chest and brings it to his mother. She opens it and finds a journal, money, and a map within. A physician called Dr. Livesey reads the map and tells them that it says that there is an enormous treasure buried on an island.

Livesey consults with his friend; a nobleman called Trelawney. Trelawney decides to buy a ship called the Hispaniola to find the treasure. He will be accompanied by a crew, Livesey as his doctor, and Jim as his cabin boy.

A few weeks later, Trelawney lets Jim meet the ship's cook, Long John Silver; a one legged-man with a talking parrot. Jim remembers Billy's warning of a one-legged pirate.

They meet Captain Smollett. Smollett doesn't like the crew and is annoyed that everybody seems to know about the treasure. Eventually, they set sail.

One day, Jim overhears Silver talking to two other men who plan to take over the ship. Silver and these men used to be pirates with Captain Flint; the pirate who owns the treasure. Jim brings this revelation to the attention of Trelawney, Livesey, and Smollett. They decide to play dumb since the pirates drastically outnumber them.

When they near the island, Silver makes his way on a boat with some of the crew and Jim. When they reach the island, Silver decides to begin the mutiny. One man refuses to join him, so Silver kills him. Jim runs deeper into the island until he meets a lunatic called Ben Gunn. Gunn used to be part of Flint's crew but was marooned on the island years ago. Gunn tells Jim that he will help him get away from the pirates if Gunn can go home with them and have part of the treasure. The rest of Jim's group make their way to the island. They take shelter in a fort built by Flint's crew years ago. At night, Jim joins his friends.

The next morning, Silver offers a truce to Jim's group. They refuse and so, Silver launches an attack. Livesey starts looking for Gunn. Jim runs off and when he returns, he sees that Silver has made his way onto the island and has taken over the fort.

The pirates want to kill Jim, but Silver says it would be better to keep him as a hostage. The pirates are infuriated with this decision and are about to slay Silver. Luckily, they stop when Silver shows them the treasure map. Knowing that he is as good as dead once the chest is located, Silver allies with Jim and his crew.

They locate the treasure site but learn that it has already been excavated and the treasure is gone. Out of frustration, two pirates attack Silver but Jim's crew shoot them, causing them to scatter. It turns out that Gunn found the treasure ages ago and took it to his cave. Silver and Jim's crew make their way to the cave and locate the treasure. They bring the treasure to the ship and journey home. At the first port, Silver steals a bag of money and flees. The rest of the crew head home and divide the treasure evenly amongst themselves. Jim tells people that there is more treasure on the island but he has no intention of going back.

55.
The Adventures of Huckleberry Finn
by Mark Twain
1884

Huck tires of his civilized life, so he takes a raft down the Mississippi river to start life anew.

The novel begins with a 13-year-old uncivilized boy called Huckleberry Finn talking to his friend, Tom Sawyer. He tells Tom how his guardian, Widow Douglas, and her sister, Miss Watson are trying to civilize him with religion. At night, Huck runs away to join Tom and other friends where they tell stories and pretend to be robbers.

Huck's abusive father, Pap, tracks down Huck and kidnaps him. He brings Huck to a cabin in the woods where he beats him. While Pap attends to other business, Huck escapes and heads down the river. He reaches Jackson's Island and settles there. He meets Miss Watson's slave, Jim, who has run away after he overheard her say he was to be sold to ruthless slave owners. Jim intends to move to a place called Cairo in Illnois where he will buy his enslaved family's freedom.

The two journey down the river on a raft and they find a house floating down the river. They enter the house and find a naked corpse. When Jim sees the corpse's face, he tells Huck not to look at it.

Huck is curious about what's happening at home, so he dresses like a girl and enters the house of a woman who has only moved into the area. He learns that the community believe Huck is dead. Worse still, Jim is the only suspect and there is a reward for his capture. Huck returns to Jim and warns him that he is being hunted. They flee using the raft.

As they travel on, their raft collides into a ship, separating Jim and Huck. A rich family called the Grangerfords shelter Huck. They have a son called Buck who befriends Huck. The Grangerfords inform Huck that they are in a 30-year blood feud against the Shepherdsons. The feud reached its peak when Buck's sister elopes with one of the Shepherdsons. This instigates a gunfight where all of the Grangerford males are shot and killed, including Buck.

Huck runs away and meets Jim who has fixed the raft. As they travel, they pick up two drifters. The drifters devise schemes against unsuspecting victims to obtain cash. When Huck leaves the drifters with Jim, he returns to learn that they have sold Jim to plantation owners called the Phelps.

When Huck arrives at their house, they assume he is a nephew whom they were expecting anyway. It turns out that the nephew Huck is pretending to be is actually Tom Sawyer!

Huck meets Tom shortly after and tells him what's happening. Tom pretends to be his half-brother, Sid while Huck continues to play the part of Tom.

Tom finds Jim and has him freed. In the process of freeing Jim, Tom gets shot by one of the Phelps. Jim has the opportunity to escape but stays with Tom until a doctor arrives to look after Jim. Later, Tom's aunt, Polly reveals the boys' real identities. It is revealed that Miss Watson died two months earlier and she freed Jim from slavery in her will.

Jim then tells Huck that the corpse they found in the floating house was his father, Pap. This means that Huck can return home. Huck doesn't want to go back home where his adopted mother expects him to be civilized so he decides to travel to the West.

56.
Dr. Jekyll and Mr. Hyde
by Robert Louis Stevenson
1866

A doctor is tormented by the monstrous Mister Hyde.

A lawyer called John Utterson is on his weekly walk with his friend, Enfield. Enfield tells Utterson how he saw a sinister man called Edward Hyde trampling on a little girl. Enfield caught Hyde and he was forced to pay the girl's family £100 to avoid a scandal.

Hyde pays most of the money with a cheque in the name of Utterson's friend, Dr. Henry Jekyll. Jekyll has changed his will suddenly so that Hyde will inherit all of Jekyll's possessions.

Jekyll is a respected gentleman in the community who would never associate with a man like Hyde. Utterson concludes's that Hyde must be blackmailing the good doctor.

Utterson tracks down Hyde to confront him. He can see that Hyde is a 4ft-tall, ape-like, deformed man and Utterson is repulsed by his appearance.

Utterson meets up with Jekyll to discuss his bizarre relationship with Hyde. Jekyll becomes terrified at the mention of the man but assures Utterson that there is nothing to worry about.

A year later, Hyde beats a man called Mr. Carew to death with a cane. At the time of his death, Carew had an envelope addressed to his friend, Utterson.

Utterson and the police find where Hyde was staying but he is nowhere to be seen. They find the murder weapon – the half-broken cane. Utterson recognizes that it is the same cane he gave to Jekyll as a gift.

Utterson meets with Jekyll once more. The doctor seems calmer and he assures Utterson that he no longer has any relationship with Hyde. Jekyll shows his friend a letter from Hyde who has departed and he apologises for all of the trouble he caused.

Utterson brings the letter to his home and his clerk points out that Hyde's handwriting is similar to Jekyll's.

Months pass and Jekyll reverts back to his old happy self. This only lasts a limited time as Jekyll suddenly acts more paranoid than ever and he starts turning away all of his friends.

Jekyll's butler, Poole visits Utterson, desperately asking for his help. Jekyll has locked himself in his laboratory for weeks and Poole is worried for his master's health.

Utterson and Poole make their way to the locked door of Jekyll's lab. They hear a voice that is not the doctor's and decide to break down the door.

They burst into the room to find the body of Hyde wearing Jekyll's clothes. Hyde is dead from an apparent suicide. They find a letter from Jekyll explaining everything.

It seems that Jekyll had concocted a potion that could transform his appearance and personality. This potion transmogrified him into Hyde. Jekyll had done horrible things in the past (it's never explained specifically what they were) and he would drink the potion to turn into Hyde so that he could indulge his wicked ways without getting detected.

At first, the transformations happened when Jekyll drank the potion, but they suddenly started to happen in his sleep.

When he started to turn into Hyde while he was conscious, Jekyll realized that Hyde would soon become the dominant personality forever. While he still had some control, Jekyll decided to take his own life in an attempt to kill the monster he created.

57.
The Picture of Dorian Gray
by Oscar Wilde
1891

A corrupt young man seems to be eternally youthful but owns a mysterious painting that reveals his true inner ugliness.

The story takes place in Victorian England. Lord Henry Wotton is watching an artist called Basil Hailward painting the young and beautiful Dorian Gray. Wotton discusses his cynical view of the world and tells Dorian that beauty is only temporary so he should enjoy it while it lasts. With this revelation, Dorian says he wishes that his portrait would age instead of him.

Later, Dorian pursues an actress called Sibyl Vane who performs in a Shakespeare play in a tattered theatre. Dorian believes that the lead actress, Sibyl Vane is such an incredibly talented actress that he falls passionately in love with her. When he meets her after the play, his beauty captivates her. Sibyl is instantly smitten with him but her brother, James threatens to kill Dorian if he ever hurts her.

Sibyl has never experienced love outside of romantic plays and she sees no need to pretend to be in love in theatre when she has experienced the real thing. Now that she has abandoned her passion, Dorian no longer finds Sibyl attractive and leaves her. Dorian returns home, noticing that the painting of himself has changed slightly. Seeing it as a bad omen, he decides to apologise to Sibyl. Lord Wotton tells Dorian that Sibyl has committed suicide.

Over the next 18 years, Dorian embraces and indulges in every sin he can experience. As Dorian is about to leave for Paris, Basil meets with him. Basil has heard that Dorian has become obsessed with sensualism; gaining knowledge by fulfilling all of the human senses. Dorian shows him what led to this obsession by taking him to a locked room. Within, he reveals the portrait that Basil painted of him. The painting has aged horrifically instead of Dorian who hasn't aged a day. Dorian believes that Basil is responsible for his curse and stabs him to death.

To avoid feeling guilty, Dorian goes to an opium den to lose himself in drugs. He's oblivious that Sibyl's overprotective brother, James is present. When James realizes that Dorian is there, he tries to shoot him. Dorian explains that he can't be the man who caused Sibyl's death because it was 18 years ago and Dorian would've been too young. James can see how youthful Dorian looks and realizes that he couldn't be the same man that caused Sibyl's suicide. As Dorian leaves, a woman confronts James and informs him that Dorian Gray is the same man that drove Sibyl to suicide. James runs after Dorian but he escapes.

One night, Dorian notices that James is hanging around his home. Dorian becomes terrified that he is going to be killed but then hears that James has been shot dead during a shooting party.

Dorian meets up with Lord Wotton and vows to be a good man from now on. At this time, Dorian is seeing Hetty Merton and he promises not to break her heart.

Now that he has embraced good, Dorian wonders if his painting is starting to revert back to normal. When he looks at the picture, he sees that it looks more disgusting than ever.

In a fit of rage, Dorian takes the knife that he killed Basil with and jabs it into the painting.

The servants of the house hear a scream and run to Dorian's secret room. They find an old man on the floor who has been stabbed through the heart. They don't know who he is until they recognize he is wearing Dorian's rings. They see that he is lying beside a painting of a young and beautiful Dorian Gray.

58.
The Time Machine
by HG Wells
1895

A scientist builds a time machine and timetravels far into the future to see what will become of humanity.

The story revolves around a scientist in Victorian England who is known as the Time Traveller. The novel begins with him educating his dinner guests about how time-travel is not only possible but how he has built a time machine himself. He returns to his guests a week later, telling them that he has travelled into the future. He then divulges his adventure.

The story then switches to the Traveller's journey in the year 802701 AD. Here, he meets the Eloi; a group of innocent, small, graceful people. They live off fruit and settle in large buildings that look futuristic, but they have been deteriorating for centuries. He finds it difficult to speak to them, as they don't seem to have any curiosity or need for knowledge. The Traveller assumes they are like this because humanity has conquered everything with technology, leaving human beings no reason to desire or learn anything else.

The Traveller returns to where he left his Time Machine, which is now missing. He learns that an unknown group dragged it into a Sphinx-like structure. The building is locked but the Traveller knows they can't use it because he removed its levers.

That night, he sees a sinister ape-like caveman descending down a cave. The Traveller follows this creature until he finds that a subterranean race called the Morlocks live underground. It turns out that humanity had split into two species – the Eloi and the Morlocks. The Traveller learns that the Morlocks have technology that makes the peaceful surface possible. He realizes that his theory about the Eloi was wrong. The hardworking lower class evolved into the light-fearing, bitter and resentful Morlocks. The rich didn't have any worries so evolved into the Eloi; a race whose thirst for knowledge had vanished.

As he explores the tunnels, the Traveller discovers that the Morlocks live off the Eloi. The Traveller no longer sees the Eloi and Morlocks as rich and poor. The Morlocks are more like ranchers and the Eloi are like cattle fattened for slaughter. He deduces that the Morlocks must've stolen his time machine.

Later, an Eloi called Weena starts drowning. None of the other Eloi try to save her nor do they care. The Traveller rescues her and Weena starts to develop feelings for him. He intends to take Weena back to his time. He forges a weapon against the Morlocks so that he can retrieve his Time Machine.

On the way back to the Eloi, the Morlocks ambush the Traveller and Weena. The Morlocks believe they can trap the Traveller in the Time Machine, not knowing its true purpose. As they take the Traveller to their domain in the Sphinx and put him inside the Time Machine, he reattaches the levers and escapes through time.

He travels 30 million years into the future. He appears on a dying Earth, completely covered in vegetation. The inhabitants of the world seem to be crab-like creatures chasing massive butterflies through blood-coloured beaches. The Traveller keeps jumping ahead in time, watching the Sun grow larger and redder until he witnesses the world die.

He returns back to his time in Victorian England, three hours after he originally left. Naturally, his visitors don't believe him but the Traveller presents some flowers Weena gave him. They are unlike anything else in the world…at least for now.

The following day, the Traveller announces that he will time-travel again and return within a half hour. Three years pass and the Traveller has yet to be heard from.

59.
<u>The Importance of Being Earnest</u>
by Oscar Wilde
1895

Two gentlemen try to fool an aristocratic family under the same alias.

The play begins with Algernon Moncrieff who is about to meet his friend, whom he believes is called Ernest. He has come to propose to Algernon's cousin, Gwendolen Fairfax. Algernon rejects this idea unless Ernest explains why his cigarette case bears the inscription, "From little Cecily, with her fondest love to her dear Uncle Jack." Ernest admits that he lives a double life and his real name is John Worthing. In the country, he is a guardian to Cecily after her late grandfather found and adopted him. Cecily knows him by his nickname, Jack,

When he wants to get away from his country home, Jack pretends to visit his fictitious brother, Ernest, in London. When he is in London, Jack takes on the persona of Ernest who leads a scandalous life. Algernon admits to a deception of his own: when he has an unwanted guest coming, he says he has to meet his non-existant friend, Bunbury. Algernon enquires about Jack's estate, but he refuses to tell him anything.

Gwendolen and her intimidating mother, Lady Bracknell enter the room. Algernon brings Bracknell into another room to give Jack the chance to propose to Gwendolen. Gwendolen accepts and emphasizes how much she loves him because his name is Ernest. To make sure she never learns of his true name (or true nature for that matter,) Jack decides to officially change his name to Ernest.

When Bracknell learns of the proposal, she interviews (or politely interrogates) Jack to see if he is worthy of Gwendolen. Brackwell seems to be won over by his charm until she learns that Jack was discovered as a baby in a handbag. Outraged, she insists that he has no further contact with her daughter.

Jack gives his address to Gwendolen, not knowing that Algernon can hear him and he writes the location to his estate on his sleeve.

Back at the estate, Cecily is studying with her governess, Miss Prism. Curious about Jack's other life, Algernon drops by and pretends that he is Jack's brother, Ernest Worthing. Gwendolen is fascinated to finally meet Uncle Jack's mysterious brother. She loves the name, Ernest and instantly falls for him. Algernon decides to also change his name to Ernest.

Jack has decided to cease his Ernest persona. He enters his estate, pretending that he is devastated at the news of his dead brother, Ernest. His plan is foiled once he realizes that Algernon has already introduced himself to Cecily as Ernest.

Gwendolen enters Jack's estate, having run away from home. She meets Cecily and they realize that they are both engaged to "Ernest." When Jack and Algernon arrive, their lie is exposed. In pursuit of her daughter, Lady Bracknell arrives.

Miss Prism enters the room and Bracknell is astonished to recognize her as a family nursemaid for her late sister 28 years ago. The last time she saw Prism, she took a baby in a carriage and never returned. Prism explains that she was writing a manuscript and while she was at Victoria Station, she absentmindedly put the novel in the baby carriage and the baby in her handbag. Bracknell realizes that Jack is this baby. This makes Jack the nephew of Lady Bracknell as well as Algernon's brother. Due to this revelation, Bracknell allows him to marry Gwendolen.

Gwendolen points out that she can only marry a man whose name is Ernest. Bracknell points out that he was named after his father who was also miraculously called Ernest!

60.
The Island of Doctor Moreau
by HG Wells
1896

A man finds himself on a mysterious island where a doctor is performing unspeakable experiments on animals.

Edward Prendick is an English gentleman who is shipwrecked until another ship picks him up. This ship is captained by a man called Montgomery. He makes a stop at a nearby island called Noble's Island. Montgomery has a beastlike servant called M'ling and his ship is full of animals. As the ship reaches Noble's Island, Prendick learns that it is owned by Dr. Moreau; an infamous physiologist whose reputation was destroyed when his grotesque experiments on animals were exposed. When he meets Moreau, the doctor is about to perform an experiment on a puma. The animal's cry makes Prendich uncomfortable and he leaves to wander the jungle. On his walk, he meets a group of people that look pig-like. As he walks back, Prendick realizes that he is being followed by a mysterious figure. Prendick runs but the figure catches up and pounces on him. Prendick sees that his attacker is a leopard-man hybrid. He whacks the creature with a stone and makes his way back to the enclosure.

The following morning, Prendick wanders by Moreau's quarters and sees that the operating room is unlocked. He enters to see a bandaged humanoid creature and an agitated Moreau who forces Prendick out. Prendick reasons that Moreau is carrying out experiments on humans and that he himself will be the next test subject. He flees into the jungle and meets an ape-man who takes him to a colony of human-animal hybrids.

The colony leader is a grey creature called Sayer of the Law. The colony worship Moreau and they have forbidden all animalistic behavior.

Moreau interrupts the colony as he is searching for Prendick. Prendick makes his way to the ocean in an attempt to drown himself to avoid Moreau turning him into a hybrid.

But Moreau finds Prendick and educates him about the pack that the hybrids (called the Beast Folk) were animals, not humans. Moreau says he is trying to transform an animal into a human, but his subjects inevitably revert back to animals.

A few days later, Prendick and Montgomery encounter a half-eaten rabbit. Knowing it is forbidden for the Beast Folk to act like wild animals, Moreau calls an assembly. He learns that the Leopard Man that attacked Prendick is responsible for eating the rabbit. The Leopard Man knows that he will endure more excruciating surgical procedures, so he escapes. The Beast Folk track him down but Prendick shoots him to give him a merciful death rather than an agonizing one on the operating table.

Over time, the puma gets loose from the lab. Moreau tries to hunt it down, but the puma kills him. Not knowing how the Beast Folk will function without Moreau, Montgomery decides to give the Beast Folk alcohol. Unsurprisingly, this makes the Folk incapable of keeping their primal urges in check and they kill Montgomery.

With no way off the island, Prendick has no choice but to live with the Beast Folk. Months go by and Prendick can see them reverting back to their animalistic ways. Prendick knows that he has little time before the Folk see him as their next meal.

Luckily, a boat happens to drift to the shore. Prendick boards the boat and is rescued three days later.

When he arrives back in England, Prendick no longer feels comfortable around humans, terrified that they will one day revert to their animal forms. He moves to the countryside where he lives in solitude.

61.
The Seagull
by Anton Chekhov
1896

The son of a fading actress tries and fails to make a name for himself in the acting community.

The play begins in the estate of Sorin; a brother of the famous actress, Arkadina. Arkadina is watching a play that she hates which was written and directed by her son, Konstantin. Konstantin is well-known because his mother is a famous actress, but he wants to be recognized for his own talent. The play's star is Nina; an overly ambitious girl whom Konstantin fancies.

Sorin's estate is managed by Shamrayev whose daughter, Masha, is in love with Konstantin. Shamrayev encourages her to woo a teacher called Medvedenko but she refuses.

Konstantin's play goes horrifically and Arkadia starts chatting to her friends in the audience. Konstantin ends the show abruptly and storms off. Few people take Konstantin seriously but the local physician, Dorn highly respects him.

Konstantin tells Sorin of his insecurities about the play when Nina enters. Konstantin kisses her and confesses that he has feelings for her, but she doesn't return his love. He wonders why Sorin keeps coming to the estate if she's not interested in him and she says that the estate's beautiful lake attracts her "like a seagull." Several days later, Arkadina gets into an argument with Shamrayev and she storms out.

Konstantin presents a dead seagull that he shot to Nina. She is horrified by this "gift." Arkadia's lover, Trigorin enters as Konstantin leaves. Nina asks Trigorin what it's like to be a writer. He says it's a difficult job. Trigorin notices the dead seagull and says that he will try to write about it. Trigorin's passion makes Nina fall in love with him.

The story jumps ahead where Arkadina and Trigorin have decided to part ways and Trigorin will be leaving that day. Konstantin shot himself in the head after suffering one humiliation too many. Nina walks up to Trigorin as he eats breakfast and offers him a medallion. On this medallion, it reads, "If you ever need my life, come and take it." It is a line from one of Trigorin's books. Arkadia enters with her brother, Sorin. Sorin has become increasingly ill over the last few months. They engage in an argument until Sorin collapses. Medvedenko makes sure he's okay.

Konstantin enters and asks Arkadina to change his bandage. As she tends to her son, Trigorin prepares to leave the house for good. Konstantin insults him, which instigates another argument. Trigorin leaves for Moscow but, before he does, Nina decides to follow her dream as an actress and goes with him believing she will become a huge star.

Two years later, Masha has gotten engaged to Medvedenko and has borne his child. In spite of her relationship, she still loves Konstantin.

Nina and Trigorin lived together in Moscow. They had a child together but lost it. Shortly after that, Trigorin went back to Arkadina. Nina never had much success as an actress and is currently travelling throughout Russia in a small theatre company.

Sorin's health continues to deteriorate and the family believe he has only days left to live. They all spend time with him except Konstantin who is working on a manuscript. Later, Nina suddenly enters and tells Konstantin that she left her amateur company. He encourages her to stay but she doesn't listen. After she leaves, Konstantin tears his manuscript in anger. As the rest of the family play bingo, they hear a gunshot. Dorn goes to investigate and learns that Konstantin has killed himself.

62.
Dracula
by Bram Stoker
1897

A Translyvanian vampire moves to London to find new victims but he must battle against the great Van Helsing.

Jonathan Harker has just become a lawyer. He ventures to Transylvania to do business with his first client, Count Dracula. Harker hopes he can sell Dracula a residence in London. He meets Dracula at his castle. Dracula is a tall old man with a white moustache, pure white skin, pointy ears, and sharp teeth.

One day, Dracula interrupts Harker while he is shaving. As Harker cuts himself, he notices Dracula is drawn to his blood. Harker can see Dracula has no reflection in the mirror.

Harker gets scared and tries to examine the house but notices that every door he tries to open is locked. He realizes that he is a prisoner in Dracula's castle.

Wandering the house, Harker meets three female vampires called The Sisters. Before they have a chance to feed on him, Dracula appears and strikes one of the women. He berates them for interfering with his guest. Dracula then informs Harker that he will be leaving for a short time on "business."

When he sees Dracula outside the castle climbing a vertical surface upside down in a reptilian manner, Harker escapes by climbing down the castle wall. He hopes to return home to his fiancée, Mina.

Mina's friend, Lucy has accepted a marriage proposal from Arthur Holmwood. Dr. Seward and Quincey Morris also propose to Lucy, but she turned them down.

Dracula makes his way to England by stowing away on a ship. He picks off the crew one by one, drinking their blood. By the time the ship arrives into England, the entire crew is dead.

Dracula tracks down Lucy, seduces her, and feeds off her blood. Lucy becomes ill and Seward asks his former teacher, Abraham Van Helsing to inspect her. Van Helsing determines the cause of Lucy's illness to be from a vampire bite, but he keeps the information to himself. Van Helsing insists that they cover her bedchamber with garlic, knowing it weakens vampires.

Mina finds out that Harker is in Budapest recovering from a mental breakdown. She goes to him, and the two get married.

Lucy's mother enters her daughter's bedroom. She removes the garlic, oblivious to its purpose. Dracula attacks Lucy and her mother in the form of a wolf. Lucy's mother dies of shock. Lucy perishes shortly after.

In the newspapers, there are reports of children being stalked in the night by a beautiful lady. Van Helsing knows this woman is Lucy, who is now a vampire. He reveals this fact to the men, and they decide to kill her. The men track down Lucy and Van Helsing stabs her through the heart with a wooden stake, beheads her, and fills her mouth with garlic.

Shortly after, Harker and Mina arrive and join Van Helsing's group to stop Dracula.

The Van Helsing gang destroy all of Dracula's lairs throughout London, which forces the Count to return to Transylvania.

Van Helsing and the others follow him to his castle. They battle against Dracula's gypsy guards and female vampires until all that is left is Dracula himself. Harker stabs Dracula in the throat and Quincey stabs him in the heart. Dracula crumbles to dust. Quincey dies from his wounds. Harker and his wife eventually have a son whom they call Quincey.

63.
The Invisible Man
by HG Wells
1897

A mysterious bandaged man comes into an inn and the inhabitants are curious to learn more of this enigmatic stranger.

During a blizzard, a heavily bandaged man called Griffin enters a local inn in West Sussex in England. Griffin wears a long coat, a hat, gloves, and has bandages completely covering his face so no part of his skin can be seen.

Anytime the locals try to speak to him, he is rude, angry, and dismissive. He devotes most of his time in his room, working with laboratory chemicals and only ventures out at night. Over time, his eccentric nature becomes the talk of the town.

Eventually, Griffin runs out of money. When his landlady demands that he pay his bill, Griffin takes off some of his bandages to reveal that he is completely invisible. Upon learning of his invisibility, the locals try to grab Griffin. With no choice, he discards his garments and flees.

He eventually meets a tramp called Thomas Marvel and convinces him to become his assistant. Griffin returns to the village with Marvel to collect his three notebooks. These books have all of the data he needs to become visible again.

Realising that Griffin is insane, Marvel runs to the police the first chance he gets. He alerts them to the Invisible Man and demands to be locked in a high security jail so Griffin can't kill him.

Griffin vows vengeance upon Marvel and attempts to kill him in his cell but is shot in the process. Griffin recovers from his wounds in a shelter. The shelter is beside a house owned by Griffin's old friend from medical school, Dr. Kemp.

Griffin confronts Kemp and reveals himself. He reminds Kemp that they went to the same school. Griffin confesses that he created a medicine that can render an object invisible. He decided to test the medicine on himself and has been unable to reverse the experiment. Frustrated by his situation, he intends to create a Reign of Terror on the entire nation with his newfound power.

Kemp goes to the police the first chance he gets to alert them of Griffin. When they arrive, they try to attack Griffin but he escapes.

The following day, Kemp finds a note from Griffin that informs him that he will be the first person to die in his Reign of Terror. Kemp believes that he should be used as bait and the locals should attack Griffin as he closes in on the doctor.

That night, a policeman guards Kemp's house. Griffin shoots him dead and then breaks into Kemp's house. Kemp runs out and makes his way to the town. Griffin is seized by the locals and killed.

As Griffin dies, his body becomes visible again. A policeman asks for his face to be covered.

In the final chapter, we learn that Marvel is in possession of all of Griffin's notes suggesting that he will become invisible in another tale.

64.
Heart of Darkness
by Joseph Conrad
1899

A sailor explores Africa during its British colonization and bears witness to the darkest side of humanity.

Marlow is a sailor on a boat on the river Thames, telling his men how he came to be the captain of a steamboat for an ivory company. As he made his way to Africa several months ago, Marlow arrived at the First Company Station. Marlow was stranded at this station for ten days before he heard about the mysterious Kurtz. Kurtz worked for a European trading company. He sought ivory in Africa, but Kurtz believed the people were savages and he could civilize them by bringing European culture to Africa. However, his time in Africa supposedly turned him into a savage himself.

As Marlow moved onto the Central Station, he learned that the steamboat he needed to explore Africa had been wrecked two days ago and would take three months to repair.

He learned that Kurtz had more success with supplying ivory than all of the other workers combined. He is envied more than he is admired. This made Marlow realize that the British were not in Africa to civilize the Africans but to steal their wealth.

Months passed and the ship was repaired. On board were Marlow, a manager, three or four pilgrims, and 20 natives that Marlow called "cannibals." It took two months to get to Kurtz's station. On the way, his ship was attacked with arrows from the jungle. Marlow blew the whistle on the ship, which made the attackers stop. One of the natives died in the attack.

Marlow remembered what it said in Kurtz's reports. Kurtz wrote that the uncivilized natives had rarely seen a white man and so would see him as a divine being. Because of this, Kurtz believed he could control the natives and bring peace. Kurtz wrote this when he was still stable. As he became unbalanced, he wrote notes saying, "Exterminate the brutes!"

Marlow arrived at Kurtz's station and saw a man waving at him. He was a Russian wanderer and he told Marlow how the natives worship Kurtz like a god. The Russian greatly respected Kurtz but worried about his recent ill health. Marlow learned that Kurtz used the tribe to raid other villages for ivory, which was then sent to the Central Station. Marlow saw a station house in the distance surrounded by human heads impaled on spikes. Marlow quickly speculated that Kurtz had gone mad.

Around the corner of this house, Marlow saw the manager and the pilgrims carrying a very ill Kurtz on a stretcher to the ship and putting him in one of the cabins. That night, Kurtz abandoned the ship to return to his house, but he was too ill. Marlow found him and pleaded with him to return to the ship. Although Kurtz was threatening, Marlow stood his ground and Kurtz agreed to return to the ship.

They left the next day. Kurtz's health worsened. The ship broke down again and as it was being repaired, Kurtz gave Marlow a photograph of a woman and some papers. His dying words were, "The horror! The horror!" before perishing.

As Marlow returned to Europe, a company representative visited him. The representative said that he was entitled to Kurtz's documents. Marlow gave him some papers but tore off the bit reading, "Exterminate the brutes!"

Kurtz had mentioned that he had a fiancée and so, Marlow visited her. It was the same woman in the photograph that Kurtz gave to Marlow. He returned the picture to her as well as some personal letters. The woman asked Marlow what Kurtz's last words were. Marlow lied and said it was her name.

65.
The Three Sisters
by Anton Chekhov
1901

The Prozoroff sisters each have their own dreams and yet, they all live unfulfilled lives.

The play revolves around three sisters from Moscow – Olga, Masha, and Irina. Olga is a teacher and she is the eldest sister. She is the matriarch of her house and looks after her sisters like a mother.

Masha is the middle child and she has been married to a schoolteacher called Feodor for seven years. Masha was very young when she married him but over the years, she sees how immature and distant he is.

Irina is the youngest sister. The girls left Moscow 11 years ago but Irina fantasises about returning there and meeting her future husband. She has two men pursuing her; a very unattractive man called Tuzenbach and a social misfit called Solyony. She is not interested in either of them.

The sisters have a brother called Andrei whom they idolize. He is in love with a poor girl called Natasha whom the sisters believe is beneath him.

The story begins with the anniversary of their father's death. Andrei admits to Natasha that he loves her. He asks her to marry him, which she accepts.

Two years pass and the story picks up with Andrei and Natasha now married with a child called Bobik. Natasha is having an affair with Protopopov who works above Andrei.

Masha arrives home after meeting Lieutenant Vershinin who knew her father. She and Vershinin secretly harbor feelings for each other.

One year later, Andrei finds himself heavily in debt due to his gambling and has no choice but to remortgage his house. His sisters are outraged at him. Further tension is created when Natasha makes herself the matriarch of the household by being cruel to the sisters' nurse, Anfias. On top of that, she forces Olga and Irina to share a room so she could take one of their rooms for her child. Masha admits to Olga and Irina that she loves Vershinin.

Irina grows upset that her teaching job feels trivial and she still hasn't met her true love. She decides to marry Tuzenbach even though she doesn't love him.

A friend called Chebutykin drunkenly stumbles into the room and smashes into a precious clock that belonged to the sisters' mother. Andrei shouts at Chebutykin for his buffoonery. Andrei apologises to his sisters for losing his temper and then apologises for allowing Natasha to take over the house and for remortgaging the house.

Later, Solyony challenges Tuzenbach to a pistol duel for stealing his love, Irina. Tuzenbach wants to hide this fact from Irina but he decides to go along with the duel when Irina confesses that she can never love him. Solyony and Tuzenbach engage in the duel and Tuzenbach is shot and killed.

Masha is devastated when she learns that Vershinin is to be transferred. Feodor is aware of her feelings towards Vershinin, but he forgives her.

Olga is promoted to headmistress and is preparing to move out. She is taking Anfisa with her to stop her from being mistreated by Natasha any further.

Irina is still devastated by Tuzenbach's death, but she decides to continue working as a teacher.

Andrei realizes that he is trapped in a loveless marriage.

66.
Nostromo
by Joseph Conrad
1904

In the South American country of Costaguana, an admired man is commanded to secure a shipment of gold and stop any revolutionaries who might try to take it. Sadly, it doesn't go to plan.

The story takes place in a fictitious South American country of Costaguana, which is heavily based on Columbia.

Costaguana has a history of warfare, tyrannical dictators, and revolutions. However, its most recent dictator, Ribiera, has created a balance in the country. Revolutions have calmed down and the natives are at peace.

Charles Gould is a native of English ancestry who lives in the city of Sulaco. He owns a silver mine near the main port of the city. Gould hates the country's politics and corruption. Gould hopes to use his wealth to maintain stability for the future of Costaguana. However, his riches invested in the government simply create more powerful warlords, which then inspire more revolutions.

Cosaguana's stability collapses and falls back into anarchy once more. A revolutionary leader called General Montero invades the city intending to stop Gould using his silver to fund power-hungry politicians.

He commands a shipmate of a boat to take the silver offshore so it can be sold to international markets. The shipmate is an Italian man known as Giovanni Battista Fidanza, but goes by the name, Nostromo. Nostromo is respected, brave, and is considered incorruptible throughout Europe. The Costaguanans believe he is the right person to be entrusted with the silver to avoid further corruption in the nation.

With the help of a journalist called Martin Decoud, Nostromo smuggles the silver out of Costaguana.

That night, the transport containing the silver collides with another ship harboring revolutionary invaders led by Colonel Sotillo. Luckily, Nostromo and Decoud move the silver onto a lifeboat. The silver is brought to the Great Isabel Island. Nostromo has no space on the lifeboat so he swims back to Sulaco.

Decoud becomes insane after spending too much time alone on the island and he decides to take his own life. He walks into the ocean with silver in his pockets so his body will sink. He then shoots himself in the head.

As Nostromo returns to Sulaco, he tells the inhabitants that the silver was lost at sea and therefore cannot be used by any manipulative figureheads.

Nostromo believes he will be perceived as a hero but instead, finds that political leaders are exploiting his public image. Over time, he becomes resentful and bitter. He becomes self-destructive and makes night trips to the island to gradually reclaim the silver. Nostromo has no idea what happened to Decoud and becomes paranoid. Unaware that Decoud took some of the silver so his body wouldn't be found, Nostromo becomes more flustered when he notices that some of the silver is missing.

Over time, a lighthouse is built on the island, impairing Nostromo's ability to reclaim his treasure. As he attempts to take the silver, he is shot and killed, mistaken for a trespasser.

67.
The Wind in the Willows
by Kenneth Grahame
1908

A mole, a badger, and a vole try to curb their friend's wild and dangerous adventures for his own sake.

The story begins with Mole cleaning his underground home. He grows bored and ventures upwards until he reaches a river. He meets a vole called Ratty. Mole has never seen a river before so Ratty takes Mole for a ride in his rowing boat.

One day, they reach Toad Hall and meet their eccentric friend, Toad. Toad is obsessed with fads but tires of them quickly. He is currently obsessed with travelling on his horse-drawn caravan and demands that Mole and Ratty join him on a trip. As they travel, a passing car scares the horse, which causes the caravan to overturn. Mole tries to soothe the horse, but Toad suddenly becomes bored of caravans and demands a car.

Mole wants to meet Badger. Ratty knows that Badger likes to have his own space so Ratty says they will meet Badger when he is in a more sociable mood. One winter day, while Ratty is asleep, Mole ventures into the Wild Wood to meet Badger. He gets lost and after seeing some scary forest animals, he panics and hides.

Ratty awakens and realizes that Mole is gone. He tracks down Mole from his tracks and they decide to go home.

In their attempt to get home, they accidentally stumble upon Badger's home. Badger is about to go to bed but when Mole and Ratty arrive at his doorstep, he welcomes them in. Ratty gossips to Badger about Toad and tells him how Toad has crashed seven cars, has been hospitalized three times, and has been forced to pay many fines. They all decide that when the winter ends, they will stop by Toad's house and stop him from indulging in his silly obsessions.

The following summer, Badger, Ratty, and Mole confront Toad to get him to cease his dangerous escapades. Toad is stubborn and refuses to listen to them, so they decide to keep him in his house until he changes his mind. Toad manages to escape and heads into an inn for food. When he sees a car pull into the courtyard, Toad steals it as soon as he can. He drives it recklessly until the police arrest him. He is given a 20-year prison sentence.

Toad befriends one of the guards' daughter and over time, she disguises him as a washerwoman and helps him escape.

Toad makes his way onto a train and meets a man who owns a horse-drawn barge. Toad asks the barge-owner if he can hitch a ride with him. The man accepts this proposal because he needs someone to clean his clothes and he believes Toad is a washerwoman. He attempts to wash the man's clothing but screws it up. The man's wife is furious with Toad and she throws him into a canal. He steals the horse and flees.

Toad hitches a ride in a passing car, which is coincidentally the car he stole earlier. The driver doesn't recognize Toad in his disguise and allows him to drive. Behind the wheel, Toad starts driving recklessly again until he drives into a pond. Toad runs away before he is arrested. He runs into a river, which carries him right outside Ratty's house. Toad overhears Ratty talking about how Toad Hall is now controlled by weasels. Badger arrives and alerts Ratty that there is a secret passage that leads to Toad Hall. Toad joins Badger, Ratty, and Mole and they enter the tunnel to Toad Hall and spring a surprise attack on the unsuspecting weasels. With the weasels defeated, Toad holds a party and apologises for his behavior and thanks his friends for their support.

68.
Howard's End
by E.M. Forster
1910

A successful but greedy businessman refuses his deceased wife's request to donate an estate to a friend.

The story revolves around three families – the wealthy Wilcox family, a reasonably rich family called the Schlegels, and a poverty-stricken couple called Leonard and Jacky Bast.

Helen Schlegel has a brief fling with Paul Wilcox. Among the reasons for ending the relationship is the Wilcoxes' mistreatment of the the Basts for being lower class.

Helen's family learns that the Wilcoxes are moving from Howard's End to a flat opposite their own home in London. The Schlegels and Wilcoxes dread the idea of Paul and Helen seeing each other again. Luckily, Paul happens to be in Nigeria and Helen is in Germany. Over time, Helen's sister, Margaret becomes friends with Paul's mother, Ruth.

Not long afterwards, Ruth dies. She leaves a note saying that Howards End is to be donated to Margaret. However, her husband, Henry never divulges this fact to Margaret.

Helen returns home shortly after. She and Margaret bump into Henry and they discuss Leonard Bast. Henry is certain that the insurance company that Leonard works in will go bust. They encourage Leonard to find a new job before his company is shut down.

Over time, Margaret and Henry become good friends. Margaret's lease on her home suddenly expires. Henry offers to rent them a house he owns in London. Upon seeing the house, Henry asks her to marry him. She accepts his proposal.

As they prepare for their wedding, Henry's daughter, Evie gets engaged. At Evie's wedding, Helen arrives with Leonard and his wife, Jacky. Helen is angry because Leonard took Henry's advice and left his company, but he was fired from his new job. What's worse is that Leonard's old insurance company didn't go bust.

Margaret insists that Leonard should work with Henry. Henry sees that Leonard's partner, Jacky was a woman he had an affair with ten years ago. To avoid his affair becoming public knowledge, he refuses to give Leonard a job. He confides about the affair to Margaret and she forgives him.

Helen and the Basts leave the party and head to a hotel. Helen and Leonard decide to stay up and end up sleeping with each other. When Helen learns that she is pregnant, she travels to Germany to hide her pregnancy from her family and Jacky.

Henry and Margaret get married and intend to move to Sussex. They decide to store their belongings in Howard's End until the move is complete. Knowing that Helen is visiting Howard's End to collect some books, Margaret thinks it would be nice to surprise her sister. When she sees her at Howard's End and realizes she's pregnant, she is overjoyed. Helen asks if she can stay at Howard's End with Margaret. Unfortunately, Henry doesn't approve of an unmarried pregnant woman. Margaret accuses Henry of being a hypocrite due to his affair and she leaves him. Helen returns to Germany and Margaret goes with her.

Leonard decides to travel to see Margaret to tell her that he got Helen pregnant (not knowing that she is already aware.) As he makes his way to Howard's End, Henry's son, Charles confronts him. Charles beats him with the flat of a sword and a bookcase falls on him. Leonard has a heart attack and dies. Charles is jailed for manslaughter.

Henry is rattled and he returns to Margaret. The couple resolves their issues. Henry, Margaret, and Helen move into Howard's End and Henry changes his will so Margaret shall inherit the estate as his wife intended.

69.
The Metamorphosis
by Franz Kafka
1915

Gregor Samsa wakes up to discover he has turned into a bug.

Gregor Samsa is a salesman until he wakes one day and learns that he has been transformed into a bug. Samsa can't comprehend this and believes he must be dreaming.

Gregor starts stressing how unhappy he is at his job. When Gregor looks at the clock, he learns that he has overslept and is late for work. Gregor is worried that his boss won't believe that he slept in.

Gregor's mother realizes that her son has overslept. She knocks on his bedroom door to check on him. He calls to her and notices his voice has changed. Gregor still doesn't believe he is a bug.

His sister, Grete asks him to open the door. Gregor tries to get out of bed, but he realizes that he can't move. Gregor can hear that his manager and chief clerk have come to his house to check why he's absent from work.

The clerk gets angry at Gregor's delay and tells him that his recent work has been poor. Gregor tries to defend himself but his voice sounds insect-like so it's indecipherable to the human ear.

He eventually gets out of bed and opens the door. Upon witnessing his vile appearance, his mother faints and the manager rushes out of the house. Gregor tries to follow him, but his father appears and backs him into his bedroom. Out of exhaustion, Gregor falls asleep.

When he awakens, Gregor sees that bread and milk have been laid by his side. Gregor used to love milk, but he no longer has any interest in it.

The next day, Grete sees that he hasn't drunk the milk, so she routinely gives him rotting food, which Gregor devours.

With little to do, Gregor spends the day listening to his family through the walls discussing what to do with him. Now that Gregor can't work, they worry about what to do financially. His mother wants to see him, but his father and Grete won't let her.

Gregor accepts his body over time. His former life and priorities stop interesting him, and he starts climbing the walls and ceiling for amusement. Grete removes some furniture to give Gregor more space. As they take ornaments away, Gregor gets upset because they take away pictures that he finds sentimental.

When his mother sees him again, she faints once more. Grete calls his name. This is the first time anyone has referred to him by name since his transformation. Gregor runs into the kitchen and sees his father. His father chucks apples at Gregor and one of them gets lodged in a sensitive area of his back. This causes partial paralysis and he is permanently injured.

The Samsa household rent rooms to people so they can pay the bills. Gregor intentionally avoids all contact with the people living in his house.

One day, when he is feeling especially depressed, he hears Grete playing the violin. Gregor is drawn by the music and enters the room where she is entertaining the group. They are bored by her performance, but Gregor finds it beautiful. As he enters the room, the people rush out in terror.

Grete snaps and demands that they get rid of Gregor. They assume Gregor doesn't understand but he does. He goes back to his bedroom and dies.

70.
A Portrait of the Artist as a Young Man
James Joyce
1916

A young Irishman searches for knowledge during the decline of his family.

The story revolves around an Irish boy called Stephen Daedalus in the late 19th century. He tries to cast off all his identities – family, political, social, and religious to find himself as a writer.

Stephen attends Clongowes Wood College, which is run by Jesuits. Stephen is naturally intellectual but is mocked by his classmates.

During a Christmas dinner, he sees the tensions rising in Ireland politically and religiously. The nationalist political leader, Charles Stewart Parnell has died, which creates a divide in Stephen's family. This shatters Stephen's belief in Irish society.

At college, teachers become stricter as tension rises in the country. Corporal punishment is implemented. Stephen accidentally breaks his glasses and a teacher strikes him, believing he did it on purpose, so he doesn't have to commit to his studies. Stephen complains to his headmaster; a gentleman called Father Conmee who assures him that discipline will not be misused again.

His father finds himself in debt and Stephen is forced to leave college so that his family can move to Dublin.

Thanks to Father Conmee, Stephen attends a great school called Belvedere College. He is academically exceptional and is made class leader.

Stephen wins a cash prize at school but squanders it on prostitutes. He starts to neglect his father who turns to drink more and more. Because of his Catholic upbringing, he feels an overwhelming sense of guilt.

Stephen's class ventures on a religious retreat where they sit through sermons. Stephen pays extra attention to the sermon when it deals with punishment, guilt, pride and the Four Last Things (Death, Judgement, Hell, and Heaven.) He believes the sermon is just for him. He feels overwhelmed and seeks penance.

He repents for all of his sins and attends Mass every day. When the Jesuits learn of his devotion, they convince him to become a priest. Stephen is divided as to whether to follow the Church, gain knowledge, follow his family, or support his country.

His sister informs him that his family can't afford to stay in Dublin, and they will be moving again soon.

He goes for a walk on the beach and sees a beautiful woman. This woman's beauty makes him realize that he will never be able to admire beauty if he devotes himself to one sort of life. He can't fully commit to the political, religious, and social institutions of Ireland simultaneously. Whichever life he commits to, he will have to neglect the others.

Stephen moves on to university and becomes good friends with a young man called Cranly. Cranly helps Stephen formulate his theories about art.

Stephen realizes that Ireland has become too restraining for his purposes to express himself as an artist and he decides to leave.

71.
The Great Gatsby
by F. Scott Fitzgerald
1925

During the 1920s, a former veteran becomes fascinated by his eccentric millionaire neighbor.

The narrator is Nick Carraway; a graduate from Yale and a veteran from World War I. He's a salesman who wants to go into the stock business to become a bond man. He rents a small house in Long Island beside a lavish mansion owned by a reclusive millionaire called Jay Gatsby. There are huge parties at the mansion every night, but Gatsby is always absent.

One day, Nick has dinner with his cousin, Daisy Buchanan and her husband, Tom. They introduce Nick to Jordan and the two start going out shortly afterwards.

Jordan tells Nick that Tom has a mistress called Myrtle. As he returns back to his house, he sees Gatsby outside his house looking out at the water in the direction of a green light, where Daisy's house is on the other side.

Shortly after, Nick, Tom, and Myrtle travel to New York City to the apartment where Tom and Myrtle are having an affair. They have a party where Myrtle annoys Tom by saying Daisy's name repeatedly. Tom hits Myrtle so hard, he breaks her nose.

In the summer, Nick receives an invitation to Gatsby's party. He meets Jordan at the party. He is astonished to learn that Gatsby is attending the party for once. Gatsby seems charming, suave, and aloof. He has a habit of calling Nick "old sport." In spite of Gatsby's larger-than-life lifestyle, Nick is surprised that Gatsby doesn't drink alcohol. Gatsby says he remembers Nick because they were in the same division in the war. Gatsby befriends Nick and talks to him about how he inherited his family's wealth, but Nick is dubious about this.

When they were at the party, Gatsby had been talking to Jordan and she told him that Nick is Daisy's cousin. Gatsby had a relationship with Daisy five years ago and he is still completely in love with her. He has luxurious parties every night hoping they will draw Daisy back into his arms. Gatsby encourages Nick to invite Daisy to Nick's house without her knowing that Gatsby will be there. It's awkward at first, but eventually they rekindle their feelings and begin having an affair.

At this point, the reader learns who Gatsby really is. Gatsby is called James Gatz and he grew up in poverty. He couldn't marry Daisy because he had no money and he only wanted to marry her for her wealth. He didn't just want to be rich; he wanted people to believe he was always rich. He befriended a wealthy man called Dan Codie. Dan always called Gatz "old sport." This gave Gatz the idea to create a new identity called Gatsby.

Tom becomes paranoid that his wife is sleeping with Gatsby. Daisy, Nick, Jordan, and Tom meet Gatsby at his suite where Tom calls Gatsby a criminal who owes his fortune to illegally selling alcohol. Daisy decides to stay with Tom. Tom knows he has beaten Gatsby and lets him take Daisy back to her house.

Nick, Tom, and Jordan drive home but discover that the car that Daisy and Gatsby had been driving crashed into Myrtle and killed her. Daisy was driving but Gatsby takes the blame. Myrtle's husband, George assumes the driver was having an affair with his wife (but he believes the driver is Gatsby.) He enters Gatsby's mansion and shoots him while he is in his pool before killing himself. This is the only time Gatsby has ever used his pool.

Nick has a small funeral for Gatsby but nobody else attends it. He breaks up with Jordan and leaves Long Island completely disillusioned by the obsession people have with money instead of being happy.

72.
The Maltese Falcon
by Dashiell Hammett
1929

A detective takes a case to locate a priceless statuette.

Sam Spade and Miles Archer are hired by Miss Wonderly to follow Floyd Thursby. He has supposedly run off with Wonderly's sister.

That night, Spade receives a phone call informing him that Archer is dead. Spade is questioned by Sergeant Polhaus. Spade tells the sergeant that Archer was investigating Thursby. When Thursby is found dead later, Spade becomes the main suspect.

The next day, Archer's wife, Iva asks Spade if he killed Archer. Spade knows it will seem suspicious if anyone learns that he had an affair with Archer'wife. He asks her to leave.

He meets Wonderly at a hotel. Wonderly informs Spade that her real name is Brigid O' Shaughnessy and that she never had a sister. Thursby was her partner who betrayed her.

Later in the day, a man called Cairo visits Spade. He offers Spade $5,000 if he retrieves a statue known as the Maltese Falcon. When Spade says he doesn't know what Cairo's talking about, Cairo pulls a gun and demands to search Spade's office. The detective gets in a lucky shot and knocks Cairo unconscious. Brigid contacts Spade and the detective meets her. When he mentions Cairo's name, she becomes nervous and demands to meet him.

The three of them meet in Spade's apartment. It turns out that Cairo and Brigid know each other. They refer to a man simply known as "G" whom they seem terrified of. Sergeant Polhaus arrives and takes Cairo in for questioning.

The following day, Spade notices a young man is following him. The man is called Wilmer Crook and he claims to work for "G."

Shortly after that, Spade gets a call from a man called Casper Gutman ("G") who demands to meet him. They meet for a drink and Casper assures Spade that he will pay handsomely for the Falcon. Casper tells him that the statue was a gift from the Maltese King to the Spanish king, but it was lost as it was being transported. It was covered in a thick black casing to hide its priceless interior. He traced it to a Russian general called Kemidov and sent Brigid to buy the statue, but he refused to sell it. Brigid then hired Cairo to help steal the artifact. Brigid wanted the statue for herself, so she left Cairo and acquired a new partner, Floyd Thursby. Spade then realizes that Casper has spiked his drink before he passes out.

When Spade wakes up, he heads to his office. A dock captain enters the office with a package and dies from gunshot wounds. Spade opens the package, which contains the Falcon.

Brigid calls him to ask for his help. Spade sees the nearby dock has been set on fire. This is the same dock that the captain must have come from. As he heads home, he finds Cairo, Crook, Brigid, and Casper waiting. Casper offers $10,000 for the statue. Spade points out that one of them has to "take the fall" for the murders. The group force Crook to take the blame. Spade has his secretary send the statue to his apartment. Spade gives it to Casper, but he realizes it is a fake. Kemidov must have created a copy of the statue before Cairo stole it. The men leave but Brigid stays. After they exit, Spade contacts Polhaus and informs him that Casper organised the murders of the dock captain and Thursby. He tells them that it was Crook who carried out the murders.

With the police on their way, Spade asks Brigid why she killed Archer. Brigid says that she hired Archer to scare Thursby, but he was unintimidated. Brigid shot Archer with Thursby's gun, pinning the blame on him. She begs Spade not to turn her in, but he says he is just doing his job. He hands her over to the police when they arrive.

73.
Brave New World
by Aldous Huxley
1932

In the future, people are led to believe that they live in a perfect society when they actually have no control over their lives.

The world is set in a futuristic utopia where everyone is happy. Through science, humanity is mass-produced and conditioned to desire certain tasks to benefit society. Certain people are conditioned to be lower class and others are conditioned to be higher-class. Couples and natural birth don't exist in modern society.

The story focuses on a psychologist called Bernard. Bernard has one of the highest ranks in society so he should be happy. But Bernard is vocal about feeling different which fuels gossip that he was supposed to belong to the lower caste.

Bernard asks the Director if he can get permission to visit the Savage Reservation in Mexico with a girl he likes called Lenina. The Director tells Bernard that he had a bad experience with a woman there many years ago. The director warns Bernard that he is unhappy with his behavior and threatens to relocate him to Iceland.

Bernard and Lenina head to the Savage Reservation. A young white savage called John approaches Bernard and Lenina and takes them to his mother, Linda. She's happy to see civilized people and tells them how they've been mistreated for years. 20 years ago, a man called Thomas impregnated her. He lost her in a storm, and she fell down a ravine and hit her head. Some passersby saw her and brought her to the village. John was born shortly after that. Bernard realizes that this man is his Director.

Bernard asks John and Linda to return home with him knowing that he can use Linda as leverage against the Director to avoid relocation to Iceland. The four of them head back to England. Linda is revealed to the Director in front of his peers and he runs off humiliated.

John and Lenina head out one night to the Feelies (movies that engage all of the senses.) The Feelie is very romantic so Lenina is compelled to take John back to her place afterward because she wants to sleep with him. This makes John unhappy so he leaves.

John gets a phonecall informing him that his mother is in the hospital. She has taken too much Soma (a drug that makes you feel happy.) She had become addicted to the drug because she wants to forget about her past. He visits her just before she dies. Enraged, he storms out to grab a huge supply of Soma and throws it out of the window.

Bernard and his friend, Helmholtz go to the hospital to confront John. They see him in the middle of a riot. Helmholtz helps John but Bernard avoids getting involved.

Afterward, Bernard, Helmholtz, and John are sent to the Resident World Controller for Western Europe, Mustapha Mond. He explains to John why the world has to be the way it is. It is decided that Bernard and Helmholtz are to be sent to an island for people who do not fit in. Mond explains that people don't need to have feelings if they have Soma as a substitute. John says he would prefer to feel any genuine emotion rather than a joyful emotion that he knows isn't real. Bernard and Helmholtz are exiled but John isn't because Mond wants to see how a "natural birth" will affect society. John moves to a lighthouse where he whips himself to eradicate any trace of civilization within him. John's self-flagellation is caught on film and he becomes a celebrity. A crowd arrives at John's lighthouse chanting, "We want the whip." John attacks them with his whip. The crowd are unfamiliar with intense emotion and John's attack instigates them to indulge in violence and taking Soma. The following day, reporters arrive at the lighthouse to find John's body hanging from a rope.

74.
__Of Mice and Men__
by John Steinbeck
1937

A mentally disabled giant and his friend look for work during the Great Depression.

The story revolves around two migrant workers – an educated man called George Milton, and a simple giant called Lennie Small. The novel begins with the two men heading to a new area in California hoping they can settle down on their own land.

On their way, they stop at a pond. George notices that Lennie has something in his pocket and asks him what it is. Lennie reveals a mouse that he was hoping could be his pet, but it is now dead. Lennie's aunt Clara used to give him mice because he loves animals more than anything. But because Lennie keeps underestimating his brute strength, he keeps killing them by accidentally squeezing them too hard.

George worries when he sees the dead rodent. He thinks how his life would be easier if he didn't have to keep looking after Lennie. They had to leave their town because Lennie tried to stroke a pretty woman but the townspeople assumed he was assaulting her.

Lennie asks George how they are different to other people. George tells Lennie that most men are loners, but they stick together forever no matter what.

When they arrive in the new town, a ranch owner gives them a job moving barley. The boss's son, Curley is a small, petty man and he is self-conscious of his short stature. He becomes intimidated upon seeing Lennie's towering size and he starts acting like a jerk to the two men.

When he leaves, Curley's flirtatious wife attempts to seduce the two men. George isn't interested but her beauty infatuates Lennie. Lennie and George meet a nice elderly man called Candy who has a dog and works with a hard-working gentleman called Slim. Slim's dog just had some puppies so he gives one to Lennie.

As time goes by, Lennie and George's dream of having their own land seems to become a realistic possibility. Candy has offered to give them the money they need to buy a farm. Curley enters and sees Lennie smiling. Out of childish rage, he attacks Lennie. At first, Lennie doesn't fight back but eventually, he grabs Curley's fist and crushes his hand.

George leaves Lennie by himself to go off with the other ranchers. Lennie wanders into a stable and chats with a black man called Crooks who is bitter at the racist ranchers. Curley's wife appears and flirts with the men. Crooks knows what kind of person she is and asks her to leave. She threatens to have him lynched.

The next day, Lennie accidentally kills his puppy by stroking him too hard. Curley's wife enters the barn. Realizing that Lennie strokes beautiful things, she asks to have her hair stroked so she can feel beautiful. But she starts to scream when he grabs her too tightly. In a panic, he breaks her neck.

Candy finds her corpse and tells George. George realizes what happened and goes back to the pond assuming Lennie will be waiting there. When he finds Lennie there, he realizes that the ranchers will kill him. To stop him from an agonizing death, George realizes that he has to kill Lennie. As Lennie talks about his fantasies about playing with animals on the farm he will own one day, George shoots him in the back of the head.

Slim, Curley, and Candy arrive and see Lennie's body. George says he had to do it but only Candy realizes that killing Lennie was an act of mercy, not punishment.

75.
Rebecca
by Daphne de Maurier
1938

A woman marries a wealthy widower but feels haunted by his mysterious deceased wife, Rebecca.

A wealthy English widower called Maxim de Winter has seduced an innocent young woman. They get married and she moves into his Manderley estate in Cornwall.

The mansion owner has a selfish housekeeper called Mrs. Danvers. She was utterly devoted to Maxim's first wife, Rebecca, who died in a boating accident a year before Maxim met his current wife. Danvers is constantly rude to the new Mrs. de Winter and heavily implies that she can never live up to Maxim's first wife. Over time, this psychological bullying starts to break down Mrs. de Winter. She becomes paranoid and convinces herself that Maxim got married in haste but doesn't actually love her.

Mrs. de Winter attends an annual costume ball. Danvers makes her wear the same dress Rebecca wore shortly before her death.

When Maxim sees his wife in the dress, he gets very angry and demands that she change her clothes. Mrs. de Winter confronts Danvers and asks her why she is being mean to her. Danvers tells her that she firmly believes that de Winters is trying to replace Rebecca. Danvers convinces her that Maxim will never love her as much as Rebecca and she should take her own life by jumping out of the window.

The women's conversation is interrupted by a rocket outside which signals that a ship has crashed. As the shipwreck is salvaged, the divers discover another boat, which belongs to Rebecca. It turns out that the boat was intentionally sunk, leaving investigators to believe it was a suicide.

Maxim decides to tell his wife the truth. He admits that his relationship with Rebecca was a sham and they hated each other from the very beginning of their marriage. Rebecca was a cruel and self-absorbed woman who manipulated people to fall in love with her. She teased Maxim repeatedly by divulging details about all of her affairs. When she fell pregnant with another man's baby, Rebecca said that Maxim would have to raise it as his own to avoid embarrassment. Maxim snapped and shot her dead. Panicked, he put her body on a boat and sank it at sea. Mrs. de Winter is reassured to learn that Maxim does in fact love her and she doesn't have to compete with his first wife.

Although Rebecca's death is considered a suicide, her lover, Jack Favell received a letter from her the day she died. He is convinced that she didn't kill herself and he publically accuses Maxim.

A police officer investigates the claim and learns that Rebecca visited a doctor on the outskirts of London on the day she died.

They locate the doctor who tells them that Rebecca was suffering from cancer, which would have killed her within a few months. He also confirms that her uterus didn't form properly so she couldn't conceive. Mrs. de Winter deduces that Rebecca intentionally mocked Maxim, hoping he would put her out of her misery quickly rather than suffer a slow death. Realizing that Maxim is off the hook, he and his wife head back home. On the way, he calls the house, but Danvers doesn't pick up the phone.

He reaches the house to see that it has been burned down.

76.
The Grapes of Wrath
by John Steinbeck
1939

A family is forced out of their home during the Great Depression and they travel, believing they can only move onto bigger and better things.

Tom Joad is paroled from jail after serving four years for manslaughter. He returns home to Oklahoma to see his family again.

Tom meets his former priest, Jim Casy. The two men travel to Tom's old house. As Tom approaches his home, he notices that all of the farmhouses are empty except that of his old neighbor, Muley Graves. Muley tells Tom that the banks evicted all of the farmers in the area. Mulberry is the only one who refused to leave. He tells Tom that the family is staying at Uncle John's house.

The following morning, Tom and Casy make their way to Uncle John's. Tom finds that his family's crops have been destroyed by a dust storm and the family has been relying on bank loans to survive. The farm is repossessed and they head to California to seek work. They see California as a utopia where there are plenty of opportunities to get jobs. Tom is not allowed to leave the state according to his parole but he doesn't feel like he has a choice.

The Joads' optimism starts to dwindle when they realize that countless migrants are heading to California with the same fantasy that everybody can get a job there. The journey is long and they have to make camp on the way. They camp with other groups and hear about people who had to leave California because they couldn't find work. With little choice, the Joads continue on their journey.

Grandpa Joad dies before they even reach California. Grandma Joad dies soon after. They arrive in California only to be forced to live in squalid camps. Noah, the eldest Joad son and Rose Joad's husband, Connie, split from the family believing that California has nothing to offer them. Rose is devastated that Connie left her because she is pregnant.

When they arrive in California, they learn that there are jobs, but the pay is extremely low. Weedpatch Camp is a clean camp operated by a big agency that protects migrants from being harassed by Californian police.

Casy becomes a labor organizer and attempts to recruit members for a labor union. The other Joads work in a peach orchard in spite of a strike. The strike becomes violent and Tom sees Casy getting killed by a police officer. Tom snaps and kills the officer.

The remaining Joads start working on a cotton farm. Tom is now a fugitive so he needs to say goodby to his family. He promises his mother that he will get a job helping the oppressed.

The family head back to their dwelling to learn that it has been flooded by heavy rain. Rose gives birth but the baby is stillborn. The Joads have no choice but to move to higher ground and take shelter in a barn.

They find a young boy and his father in the barn dying of starvation. Now that Rose has given birth, she can produce milk. Rose offers the man her milk in order to keep him alive.

77.
The Big Sleep
by Raymond Chandler
1939

A private detective is hired by a rich family to solve a multi-layered murder.

An old, ailing general called Sternwood hires a private investigator called Philip Marlowe. A bookseller called Arthur Geiger has blackmailed Sternwood's daughter, Carmen with nude photographs of her. The suspect is Joe Brody who has blackmailed her in the past. Sternwood mentions that his daughter, Vivian is worried because her husband, Rusty is missing. Marlowe inspects Arthur's bookstore and meets the book clerk, Agnes. He learns that the bookstore is an illegal adult library. He finds Arthur's house and stakes it out until he sees Carmen show up. Shortly after, he hears a scream, gunshots, and cars. He bursts into the house to find Arthur dead and Carmen naked. The two of them are in front of a camera with no film. He takes Carmen home and returns to Arthur's house to find his body missing.

The next day, the police contact Marlowe to inform him that Sternwood's car drove off a pier. The only body found in the vehicle was that of Sternwood's chauffeur, Owen.

Marlowe waits outside the bookstore looking for any suspicious activity. He eventually sees the store's contents being transferred to the house of Joe Brody.

Vivian comes to Marlowe's office and tells him that she went to a casino that is run by Eddie Mars and she believes that his wife, Mona, ran off with Rusty.

Marlowe heads to Brody's house and finds him with Agnes. Before he has a chance to deduce their involvement, Carmen breaks in with a gun. Marlowe takes her gun and throws her out. He learns that Owen was in love with Carmen. When Owen found out that Arthur was blackmailing her, Owen killed him and took the film. Brody was staking out Arthur's house at the same time that Marlowe was and chased after Owen. Brody caught up to him, stole the film, knocked Owen out and then pushed his car off a pier.

Without warning, Brody is shot dead from an outside shooter. Marlowe catches the killer who turns out to be Arthur's male lover, Carol. He killed Brody believing that he shot Arthur. It was he that hid Arthur's body. Carol is sent to prison.

As the case winds down, Marlowe is still perplexed by one thing – Rusty is still missing. Mars calls Marlowe to his casino. Vivian is also there and Marlowe wonders about her involvement. Marlowe drives Vivian home and she tries to seduce him, but he dismisses her. He gets home and finds Carmen in his bed, but he tells her to get out.

Agnes' new partner, Harry Jones approaches Marlowe and tells him that he knows where Mona is located. Marlowe agrees to meet Harry later but Mars' bodyguard, Canino kills him. Marlowe meets Agnes who tells the detective that Mona is in a repair shop called Realito. As he enters, Canino knocks him unconscious.

He wakes up to see Mona in front of him. It turns out that Mona hasn't seen Rusty in months and Eddie invented the story that Rusty ran off with her. She is attracted to Marlowe, so she frees him. Marlowe kills Canino and then flees. Marlowe visits Sternwood's home the following day. Marlowe still has Carmen's gun that he took off her at Brody's house. When he returns it to her, she asks him to teach her how to use it. He agrees and takes her to a field. She tries to kill him, but he had loaded the gun with blanks.

Marlowe brings her back and confronts Vivian. He knows that Carmen killed Rusty when he turned down her advances and Vivian paid Canino to hide his body. Eddie created an alibi by inventing the story that his wife ran off with Rusty. Vivian vows that she did it to protect her father's reputation. She assures Marlowe that Carmen will be instituionalised.

87

78.
Animal Farm
by George Orwell
1945

The animals of a farm successfully revolt against its human owner but then some of the animals become corrupted by power.

An old boar called Major summons all of the farm animals of Manor Farm to a meeting to discuss the Humans. Major views the Humans as parasites and he rallies the animals with a revolutionary song called Beasts of England. He dies shortly after.

Two pigs, Snowball and Napoleon, assume control of the other animals by attacking Mr. Jones, the owner of Manor Farm and forcing him to run away. They celebrate the end of Jones' tyranny by renaming their home, Animal Farm.

They create Seven Commandments of Animalism including, "Whatever goes upon two legs is an enemy," "No animal shall drink alcohol," and "No animal shall kill any other animal." The most important Commandment is, "All animals are equal."

The farm becomes very successful. The pigs elevate themselves by claiming only they can maintain the farm's high standard. But Napoleon and Snowball start to have a difference in opinion. Snowball wants to build a windmill but Napoleon has the dogs run Snowball out of the farm. Napoleon declares himself the farm's leader.

As Napoleon takes charge, the ethics of the farm change. Instead of having animal meetings, the pigs make decisions in their own private meetings. They start altering the Commandments one by one changing them to, "No animal shall drink alcohol *to excess"* and "No animal shall kill any other animal *without cause."*

Napoleon and another young pig called Squealer decide to go ahead with Snowball's idea and construct a windmill. Once it is built, it is abruptly destroyed in a violent storm. Napoleon tells the animals that it was clearly sabotage caused by a jealous Snowball. Napoleon starts to have animals he believes aren't on his side killed by his dogs. A song dedicated to Napoleon replaces the original revolutionary song, Beasts of England.

Mr. Jones' neighbor, Mr. Frederick learns that Manor Farm has gotten out of control and blasts the rebuilt windmill with dynamite. The animals chase Frederick out of the farm but the workhorse Boxer is badly injured.

Boxer continues to work in spite of his injuries in an attempt to reconstruct the windmill. He eventually collapses out of exhaustion. Napoleon claims he will be sent to a vet by a van to be looked after. Benjamin the donkey notices the "vet" that takes Boxer is actually the same person who takes the ill animals to the meat factory. Squealer tries to explain to him that the vet's van used to be owned by the meat factory and he hasn't had a chance to have it repainted. In reality, Napoleon sold Boxer for money to buy whisky.

As the years go by, the pigs take on more and more human traits; walking upright, triple chins, wearing clothes, etc. The Seven Commandments have now been replaced by one Commandment, "All animals are equal, but some animals are more equal than others."

The story concludes with the pigs meeting with the neighboring farmers to form an alliance. They celebrate by playing cards as the other animals look at the game from outside the window. It turns out that everyone has started the game by playing the same card – the ace of spades. They all engage in a fullblown argument. The outside animals look at the humans and pigs and realize they can no longer distinguish which is which.

79.
All My Sons
by Arthur Miller
1947

A successful businessman learns that an unforgivable sin from his past has resurfaced.

The play focuses on a successful industrialist called Joe Keller. The story begins with Joe and his wife, Kate being visited by their neighbor, Frank. Kate's son, Larry went missing three years ago and she asks Frank to let her know what his horoscope says so she can get an idea of what Larry is up to. She believes Larry will eventually return but her other son, Chris is certain he's gone for good.

Chris intends to propose to Ann Deever; Larry's former girlfriend who he has been seeing for two years. Joe and Kate are shocked when they learn of this but Bert, the boy next door, interrupts them. He starts chatting but when he says the word "jail," Kate reacts badly.

Ann arrives soon after. Her father, Steve, is in prison for selling defective cylinders to the Air Force, which caused 21 pilots to die in plane crashes. Joe was Steve's partner, but he escaped blame. Ann admits that she and her brother, George, no longer have any communication with their father. She starts to get anxious and panics that Larry may have died due to a faulty engine.

After a heated argument, Chris breaks in and proposes to Ann. She accepts. Chris also confesses to Ann that he led a company during the war and he lost all of his men, which led him to suffer from survivor's guilt.

Chris doesn't tell his mother that he's engaged.

Their neighbor, Sue, enters and reveals that the neighborhood believe that Joe is as culpable as Steve is over the defective cylinders.

George enters and alerts everyone that he has just visited Steve in prison. George learned from his father that it was Joe who told Steve to cover the damaged cylinders and send them out anyway. Because of this, he stops Ann from marrying Chris. Joe denies George's accusations. Joe says that he couldn't have despatched the cylinders because he had the flu. Kate points out that this can't be true as Joe hasn't been ill for 15 years.

Later, Frank comes over again and says that according to Larry's horoscope, Larry should be alive.

Chris goes missing. Kate tells Joe that he must confess to his crimes once Chris returns. Joe gets angry, saying that his family are turning against him after he built his entire fortune on the cylinders.

Ann enters and tells Kate she has a letter from Larry. The letter reads that because of Joe's guilt, Larry intends to take his own life.

Upon hearing this, Joe agrees to go to the authorities. Joe says that he is going inside to get his coat. Upon entering his house, he shoots himself in the head.

At this time, Chris happens to return. When he learns what has just happened, Kate tells him not to blame himself.

80.
The Pearl
by John Steinbeck
1947

A poor man finds a precious pearl which changes his life, but not for the better.

Kino, his wife Juana, and their infant son, Coyotito live in a small house by the sea. One morning, a scorpion stings Coyotito so his parents take him to the doctor. The local doctor is an obese, arrogant white man and he dismisses Kino for being poor and black.

As Juana tends to Coyotito's wounds, Kino searches for pearls in the sea. Kino finds a large, precious pearl unlike anything he has ever seen. In his excitement, Kino lists a number of things he will buy for his family when he sells the pearl for a great fortune. The rest of the neighborhood gather at Kino's house to congratulate him.

That evening, the doctor arrives, claiming he was unavailable earlier to tend to Coyotito's wound. He administers a powder to the infant and says he will return in an hour. When the doctor leaves, Coyotito becomes increasingly ill. Kino becomes paranoid and hides the pearl under the floor in the corner. The doctor returns and feeds Coyotito a concoction to soothe his pain. When the doctor asks for payment, Kino assures him he will be paid once he sells his pearl. As he says this, he instinctively looks in the pearl's hiding place. At the pearl's mention, the doctor becomes unmistakably intrigued, increasing Kino's paranoia. That night, Kino buries the pearl under his sleeping mat. As Kino tries to sleep, he hears a burglar in his house. Kino attacks him but the burglar injures Kino before escaping. Juana orders Kino to destroy the pearl or else it will destroy them.

The following morning, Kino and Juana head into town to sell the pearl. Kino's brother, Juan Tomas, goes with them and warns them of con-artists. All of the dealers that Kino visits strategically cheat him by assuring Kino that the vast size of the pearl doesn't mean it is of a high quality. They offer him low prices, assuring him that the pearl will age badly. Kino knows he's being conned and says he will get a fair price at the capital.

That night, Kino learns that the pearl is gone. He discovers that Juana has taken the pearl to get rid of it. He tracks her down, takes the pearl back, and viciously beats her. As he returns to his house, there is a group of men who demand that Kino give them the pearl. They engage in a fight until Kino kills one of them.

Kino and Juana gather their belongings and Coyotito and prepare to leave by canoe. When Kino learns that his canoe has been destroyed, they have no choice but to walk to Juan Tomas' house. As they ascend, they can see that their house has been set on fire.

Kino's family reaches his brother's house. Juan Tomas assumed Kino died in the fire and is happy to see his family is safe.

That night, Kino, Juana, and Coyotito make their way to the capital, hoping they will get a good price for the pearl there. After a day of travelling, he realizes that three people are following him. Kino tells Juana that they must run to lose their trackers. The trackers take a break and set up camp. Two of the men sleep as one takes watch. Kino sees this as the ideal time to dispose of the trackers. Kino sneaks up on the trackers, and as he is about to pounce, Coyotito starts crying. This awakens the other trackers. One of them fires his rifle in the direction of the cry. With no time to waste, Kino kills the men quickly and efficiently. Kino returns to his wife only to learn that the gunshot struck and killed Coyotito. They return to their neighborhood, with Juana cradling her dead son. Everyone stares at them in fascination. Kino walks into the water and pulls out the pearl. He stares at it for a long time before hurling it into the sea.

81.
Nineteen Eighty-Four
by George Orwell
1949

A worker rebels against his totalitarian government by falling in love.

England is in ruins due to war and it is running low on food and clothes. Everything looks dilapidated apart from the government's towering pyramid buildings. The government calls itself Big Brother. There are posters everywhere that say, "Big Brother is Watching You." Everyone is watched everywhere through screens by the Thought Police.

Everyone must obey Big Brother's rules, or they will be sent to an intense labor camp. The law bars people from having close friends or from being in love. Television consists mostly of government-controlled news. Keeping a private diary merits the death sentence.

The story's main character is Winston Smith. He has a government job at the Ministry of Truth where he edits and revises historical records to conform with the government's version of "the truth."

Winston has a secret diary where he writes how much he hates the manipulation of the government. He ponders if life can go back to the way it was but then doubts himself since the government changed all of the history books so there is no way to know what the old days used to be like.

At work, he only knows two people; a woman called Julia with whom he is in love, and O' Brien who is a friendly boss in the Inner Party. One day, she hands him a note confessing her love for him. They illegally begin an affair and regularly meet in an antique shop, which they believe can't be monitored by Big Brother.

Shortly after that, O' Brien invites Winston to his house. Invitations out of friendship don't happen in this world so Winston assumes O' Brien is a rebel who is against everything the government stands for. He and Julia confess their love to O' Brien and their hatred for the government. O' Brien confirms that he is a rebel and he is trying to bring down Big Brother.

Not too long after, the Thought Police capture Winston and Julia in the antique shop and bring them to the Ministry of Love to be interrogated. O' Brien confesses that he concocted the Rebellion force to find anyone attempting to defy the government. Winston is tortured with electroshocks in an attempt to show him that manipulation can cure him of his "insanity."

Winston is left a broken man and admits to all crimes he is accused of whether he has committed them or not, implicating everyone he can, including Julia. Winston is psychologically broken down until he sees Big Brother as a necessary evil to fulfill the "greater good." O' Brien mocks Winston and corrects him by saying Big Brother's goal is to obtain absolute power.

O' Brien tells Winston that his interrogation isn't over because he still loves Julia. He is sent to Room 101; the most feared room in the Ministry of Love, which contains each prisoner's greatest fear. In this room, a wire cage containing starving rats is strapped to Winston's face. As the rats start to approach his face, he screams, "Do it to Julia!" betraying his love.

After being reintegrated into society, he meets Julia in a park. They admit they betrayed each other.

The novel concludes with Winston in a café listening to the news and smiling. The last line of the story is, "He loved Big Brother."

82.
Death of a Salesman
by Arthur Miller
1949

A failed salesman recognizes the emptiness in his life and tries to rectify it.

The play begins with a 63-year-old businessman called Willy Loman returning home from a cancelled business trip. At first, his wife, Linda assumes Willy's home early because he has been in a car accident again. Willy complains to his wife that their son, Biff is "a lazy bum" and hasn't made anything of his life. Biff was an athlete at school, but he failed math just before graduation and never went to college.

Biff and his brother, Happy are staying at Willy's house for now since Biff returned from a long trip. (Willy doesn't know that Biff was actually in prison.) Biff and Happy talk about how their father has grown mentally unstable and is now prone to talking to himself.

Linda tells her sons that the car crash that their father was in before was not an accident but a suicide attempt. On top of that, she found evidence in the garage that Willy has attempted to asphyxiate himself.

Willy enters and complains how lazy his sons are. To alleviate Willy's mind, Happy tells him that Biff has prepared for a job interview the following day.

Willy goes to his boss, Howard the next day. Willy wants to work in the city to save him the trouble of travelling but his boss refuses. Willy gets into an argument and gets fired. Throughout the play, Willy hallucinates and sees his dead brother, Ben. Ben found a diamond mine in a jungle decades ago and became rich. Willy decided not to go with him, and he sees Ben as living the unobtainable American Dream he so desperately craves.

Biff waits for hours to see an employer he used to work with. When the employer sees him, he doesn't remember Biff. Biff impulsively steals a pen and runs away.

Willy goes to the office of his neighbor, Charley, and runs into Charley's son, Bernard. Bernard was a geek that Willy and Biff use to mock when he was in school. Willy can now see Bernard has become a successful lawyer. Bernard tells Willy that when Biff failed math, he wanted to go to summer school, but he suddenly changed his mind. When Willy asks why, Bernard says that Biff said he was going to visit Willy in Boston. When Bernard asks Willy what happened in Boston, Willy becomes agitated.

Happy, Biff, and Willy meet in a restaurant. Biff tries to tell Willy about the failed interview, but Willy is so rattled by the day, he can't listen to anything except good news. As Biff talks, Willy's mind drifts back to his time in Boston. Willy was having an affair when Biff burst into the hotel room that Willy was staying in and caught him in the act. Biff sees that his father is a fraud and this forever changes his perception of his father.

Biff leaves the restaurant in frustration and Happy leaves with some girls he picked up. When they two boys return to the house, their mother viciously confronts them about abandoning their father at the restaurant. Willy is now outside in the garden planting seeds and talking to himself. Biff tries to apologise, but this just makes Willy angry again. Biff tells Willy that they are ordinary men who are incapable of achieving anything great. He hugs his father and begs him to let go of the idolization Willy has for Biff's potential that he can never achieve. Willy is too far-gone to understand what his son is saying. He believes that Biff has forgiven him for everything, and he wants to be a businessman. Willy gets into his car and intentionally crashes it so Biff can use the life insurance to start a business.

At the funeral, Biff says he doesn't want to become a businessman like his father. Happy agrees to follow his father's business.

83.
The Old Man and the Sea
by Ernest Hemingway
1951

A fisherman battles for three days with a huge fish that has dragged him out to sea.

A Cuban fisherman called Santiago has gone 84 days without catching a single fish. He has an apprentice called Manolin but his parents have banned him from sailing with Santiago, considering him to be useless at collecting fish.

Manolin visits Santiago's shack every night. He prepares Santiago's gear, makes his food, and obsesses about his favourite baseball player, Joe DiMaggio.

Santiago informs Manolin that he is sailing the following day into the Gulf Stream, which is north of Cuba in the Straits of Florida. He believes that his luck will turn for the better in that region.

The next day, Santiago heads to this Stream in his small skiff boat and sets his line. By noon, a monster swordfish called a marlin snags the line. It's so gargantuan that it drags Santiago's entire boat. But Santiago manages to hold on for two days. Santiago isn't angry at the beast; he's impressed. He sees it as a worthy adversary and refers to it as "brother." Out of respect, he vows that nobody shall eat this fish.

On the third day, the fish starts circling around the boat. At this point, Santiago is exhausted and delirious. As the marlin approaches, Santiago lugs the fish onto its side and stabs it with a harpoon.

He attaches the fish to the side of the boat and returns home. Pride gets the better of him and he neglects his promise not to eat the fish. He starts fantasizing about the vast price he will obtain for the marlin and how many people it will feed.

Unfortunately, sharks start approaching the boat as they are attracted by the marlin's blood. Santiago kills one shark with his harpoon but then loses his weapon. He forges a new harpoon by tying a knife to the end of an oar. He kills five sharks before the remaining sharks disperse. However, they return with some of their shark friends and continue to nibble at the marlin. By nighttime, the marlin's corpse is nearly completely devoured. All that is left is a skeleton, a backbone, a tail, and a head.

Santiago reaches shore before dawn the next day. He walks to his shack, falls into bed and goes to sleep immediately.

The next day, a bunch of fishermen inspect the marlin's skeleton. They measure it to be 18ft long. Tourists assume that it is a shark.

Manolin enters the shack and sees Santiago. Manolin was worried Santiago was lost at sea and is so overjoyed, he cries. Manolin brings him newspapers and coffee. When the old man awakens, they vow to fish together once again.

84.
Catcher in the Rye
by J.D. Salinger
1951

Holden is an adolescent feebly trying to find his place in the world.

Our story takes place in the 1940s and follows a 16-year-old from New York called Holden. He doesn't feel like he fits in anywhere. He has recently flunked out of several prestigious schools because he doesn't apply himself. The story begins at the school, Percy Prep, at a football game. He has decided to leave the school soon. Before he departs, Holden wants to say goodbye to a teacher he respects called Mr. Spencer. Spencer tells him that Holden doesn't have any ambition. Holden doesn't want to think about his future and exits.

He later bumps into a guy in Holden's dorm called Stradlater who brags about an upcoming date with Jane; a girl Holden fancies. Later, Stradlater returns from his date but acts strangely. Holden assumes he tried to grope her and the two got into a fight, with Stradlater easily winning.

Holden leaves the school immediately after and gets on a train to New York. When he arrives, he checks into the Edmond Hotel. He looks at people in opposing buildings through his window. He sees a couple spitting at each other. He accuses them of being perverts, but he is curious at their behavior.

He goes downstairs and chats to a trio of women. He buys them drinks but all he is left with is their bill. He goes to a lounge and senses that the people there are "phonies."

As he exits, the elevator operator, Maurice tells Holden that he can send a prostitute called Sunny to his room for $5. He accepts. When Sunny arrives, Holden can see how young she is and views her as a person rather than a sex object. Holden says he just wants to talk, which makes her angry. When he pays her $5, she storms off and returns with her pimp, Maurice, demanding more money. Sunny takes $5 from Holden's wallet. Before Maurice leaves, he punches Holden in the stomach.

Later, Holden telephones a girl he once dated called Sally. They liked each other although Holden is still infatuated with Jane. The following day, Holden goes on his date with Jane. He tries to be spontaneous and asks her to run away with him, which she declines. He loses his temper at Jane, which upsets her so she goes home.

Holden sneaks back into his old house to see his younger sister, Phoebe. Holden doesn't want to tell his parents he flunked out of another school. Phoebe accuses him of having no direction in life. Holden says he has a dream of children running through a field of rye and catching them before they run off a cliff. He bases this image on a line he misheard in Robert Burns song "Comin' Through the Rye."

Holden leaves and meets an old teacher called Mr. Antolini. He tells Holden that the feelings he is experiencing are common in teenagers. Holden is too exhausted to listen, so he goes to sleep. He wakes up later to find Antolini patting Holden's head. Holden freaks out and runs away. He wanders the city disorientated.

In the morning, Holden goes to his sister's school and tells her he is going to run away from society. She wants to join him, but he refuses. Feeling bad, he decides to take her to a carousel. As he sees her filled with joy, it is the only time in the story where Holden is happy.

Holden tells this tale in a tuberculosis rest home. Holden says that when he gets out, he will go to another school and apply himself for once but the book concludes with the implication that Holden hasn't much time left to enjoy any potential future.

85.
East of Eden
by John Steinbeck
1952

Cal feels his father loves his brother more than him, which turns him into a resentful, evil man.

In the late 19th century, Samuel Hamilton and his wife, Liza move from Ireland to Salinas Valley in California. His nine children are raised on rough, infertile land. Over the years, the kids grow up and leave to find their own paths.

One day, a rich man called Adam Trask and his pregnant wife, Cathy Ames buy the best ranch in the area. He becomes good friends with Samuel. Adam used to live on a farm in Connecticut with his half-brother, Charles. Charles detests Adam because his father, Cyrus always favoured Adam over him. When Cyrus died, he left a huge fortune to his sons.

Charles meets Adam's partner, Cathy and instantly takes a dislike to her. Neither men know that she used to be a prostitute who murdered her parents and stole their money. To show that he is in charge, Charles drugs Adam on his wedding night and sleeps with Cathy.

The couple move to get away from Charles. Cathy gives birth to twins, Aron and Caleb. Soon after, Cathy leaves to resume life as a prostitute. She takes control over the most popular brothel in the area. Samuel learns of Cathy's fate but hides this fact from Adam's family.

Years pass and Aron grows to be a loving, caring man like his father and Cal grows up to be a dark, reprehensible person like his mother.

Adam has become rattled since Cathy left him. To help him snap out of it, Samuel tells Adam that Cathy works at the brothel. Samuel dies shortly after. After his funeral, Adam visits the brothel. He now finds Cathy repulsive and finds it easy to get over her.

Adam moves his family into Salinas town so Cal and Aron can attend school. Aron meets a girl at the school called Abra and the two form a relationship. Cal is conflicted by his dark side but when he learns the truth about his mother, he seems to embrace his evil side even more. Adam's housekeeper, Lee encourages Cal to follow his own path rather than believe he must inherit his mother's evil.

Aron starts to devote himself to God and buries himself in religion which Lee and Abra find cowardly.

Adam spends his money on a refrigeration business that turns sour. Aron graduates and leaves for university. Adam misses Aron as he sees him as more ambitious than Cal.

Cal scams people for money, hoping to pay off his father's debt. When Aron comes home for Thanksgiving, Adam is overjoyed.

Cal thinks this is the ideal time to give Adam the money. Adam is appalled that Cal raised the money illegally and refuses to accept it. Out of petty jealousy, he drags Aron to the brothel and shows him his mother to shatter his innocent mind. Aron snaps and runs away to join the army. Cathy commits suicide after seeing Aron's reaction to her and leaves her fortune to him. Cal feels guilty and begins a relationship with Abra, which curbs his dark nature.

Adam and Cal receive a telegram informing them that Aron was killed in World War I. Adam suffers a stroke and Lee brings Cal and Abra to him as he lies on his deathbed. Lee tells Adam that Cal only told Aron about his mother because he was jealous that he was the favourite son. Adam offers his blessing to Cal and just before he dies, he says the word, "timshel" which is Hebrew for "You have the power to choose."

86.
The Crucible
by Arthur Miller
1953

During the Salem witch trials, a girl frames her ex-lover's wife as a witch, causing irreparable consequences.

The play is set in 1692 in Massachusetts. The reverend, Parris is concerned that his daughter, Betty has become ill due to witchcraft. The night before, he saw Betty dancing in the forest with his niece, Abigail, and his slave, Tituba. Parris confronts Abigail about her time in the forest. She admits she danced in the woods, but she denies practicing witchcraft.

Proctor arrives to see what all the fuss is about. He confronts Abigail and they talk about their former relationship. They stopped seeing each other once Proctor's wife, Elizabeth discovered his infidelity. Abigail dismisses his wife which makes Proctor storm off.

An exorcist called Reverend Hale arrives and inspects Betty. With Hale present, Abigail implies that Tituba called upon the Devil. Parris and Hale then threaten Tituba and she admits that she and other women in the town have experimented with witchcraft. Proctor's maid, Mary Warren joins Abigail in accusing other women in Salem.

At home, Proctor's wife urges him to tell the townspeople that Abigail's accusations are "only sport" and shouldn't be taken seriously. Mary returns home and Proctor tells her off for not helping Elizabeth. Mary responds by declaring that she no longer serves them now that she has a higher calling. Mary tells Elizabeth that her name came up during the accusations, but Mary vouched for her. As a sign of good will, Mary gives her a doll.

Hale suddenly enters. He informs them that Elizabeth's name was mentioned, and he has to investigate every person who has been accused. He asks Elizabeth if she has any poppets in the house. Elizabeth shows Hale the doll that Mary gave her. He notices that it has a needle in its center and remembers that Abigail told him that she had a stabbing pain earlier. Hale sees this as enough evidence to send Elizabeth to jail for witchcraft.

The accusations are brought to court. An elderly man called Giles Corey tells Judge Danforth that the townspeople are accusing the wealthy in an attempt to steal their property. Another man called Francis has a signed declaration from 90 people supporting women like Elizabeth. Proctor convinces Mary to confess to the court that she was lying about everyone she indicted. When Abigail and other girls arrive in the court, they accuse Mary of witchcraft. Proctor confesses that he slept with Abigail and she has concocted this scheme about Elizabeth so she can be with him instead. Abigail denies the affair.

Danforth decides to bring out Elizabeth to see if she confirms Proctor's accusation. Proctor insists that Elizabeth is so pure, she would never lie. Elizabeth assumes that the affair will destroy Proctor's reputation, so she denies it too. Danforth sees Proctor's affair as a lie to discredit Abigail. Hale tells Danforth that Proctor seems genuine and Abigail appears duplicitous. Abigail pretends to hallucinate and accuses Mary of bewitching her. Mary snaps and accuses Proctor of forcing her to write in the Devil's book. Proctor is arrested.

The next scene begins on the day that Proctor is to be hanged along with other people impeached for witchcraft. Abigail has run away with all of Parris' money. Hale speaks to the prisoners and tells them to admit to witchcraft because they cannot be hanged if they confess. Proctor decides to admit to witchcraft when he learns that Elizabeth is pregnant. But when Danforth insists that Proctor must sign his confession, Proctor refuses, knowing that it will be pinned to the church door for the entire town and his future sons to see. He can't live with the shame, so he accepts his death. The play ends as Proctor is carried away to be hanged.

87.
Fahrenheit 451
by Ray Bradbury
1953

In a world where books are outlawed, a fireman whose job is to burn books questions his place in the world.

In a dystopian future, books have been outlawed. The story revolves around a man called Guy. Guy is a "fireman," meaning he burns the possessions of people who read books.

One night, he meets his neighbor; a teenager called Clarisse. She is idealistic and doesn't compromise what she believes, which makes Guy question his morals. Clarisse goes missing soon after.

A few days later, while Guy and another fireman are destroying an old woman's book-filled house, Guy steals a book, which happens to be The Bible. The old woman refuses to leave and burns herself alive. Guy returns home and hides the book. He tries to have a meaningful conversation with his wife, Mildred, but it only makes him realize how little he knows about her.

Guy doesn't go to work the next morning. His boss, Beatty visits him to see how he is. Beatty senses Guy's concerns and reminds him that books need to be destroyed because stories force humanity to cling onto ancient ideas. He casually mentions that every fireman steals a book eventually and they will not get into trouble if they burn it within 24 hours.

As Beatty leaves, Guy reveals to Mildred that he has a stash of books. She is about to burn them, but Guy asks her to read them.

As they read, they hear a noise outside which is the Hound (an eight-legged dog robot that the firemen used to locate books.) Guy thinks that one of the books might have the answer to his problems. Since nobody is allowed to have books, most people can't read them including Guy. Guy contacts a professor called Faber who read books before they were outlawed. Guy heads to Faber's house with the Bible he stole. He gives Guy an earpiece communicator so he can speak to him when Guy is in his home.

He returns home to see that Mildred and her friends are watching television. He leaves and then re-enters with a book of poetry. Guy recites a poem, which makes Mildred's friend, Phelps cry. She begs him to burn the book, which he does. The women leave in disgust and Mildred locks herself in the bathroom and takes pills. Guy hides his books in the backyard but keeps his Bible. He heads to his workhouse and finds Beatty playing cards with other firemen. He hands them the Bible, which they immediately chuck into the bin. Suddenly, the fire alarm goes off. The men get into their truck and head to their destination – Guy's house!

Beatty informs Guy that Mildred and her friends reported him and he must burn his own house. After Guy destroys his home with a flamethrower, Beatty notices his earpiece. He now intends to hunt down Faber. Guy incinerates Beatty and runs to Faber's house. Faber encourages Guy to head to the countryside where other banished book-lovers live.

Guy heads down the countryside the next day and meets one of the book-lovers called Granger. Granger and Guy see bombers flying towards the city. The planes annihilate it with a nuclear bomb, killing everybody. Granger and Guy are rattled by the shockwave but survive.

The next day, Granger teaches Guy about the story of the legendary Phoenix who lives an eternal cycle of life, death in flames, then rebirth. Granger tells Guy that the difference between humanity and the phoenix is that when men are destroyed, they can learn from their mistakes.

88.
Waiting for Godot
by Samuel Beckett
1953

This is a play where nothing happens. Twice.

Estragon and Vladimir are two bedraggled friends. Estragon claims he was beaten the night before. The two bicker at each other childishly and pointlessly. Estragon decides to leave but Vladmir reminds him that they are waiting for Godot.

The pair are to meet Godot beside a tree and they are near the only tree in the area. Estragon suggests that they hang themselves. They eventually dismiss the idea. They ask whether it is even worth waiting for Godot. Nevertheless, they stay. Suddenly, they hear a horrible cry. A slave called Lucky arrives. Lucky has a rope tied around his neck, which is held from behind by his domineering master, Pozzo. Pozzo commands Lucky abusively but acts like a gentleman to Vladimir and Estragon.

Pozzo rests with the men and eats chicken and wine without offering any food to them. After several outbursts to Lucky, Vladimir snaps at Pozzo for his mistreatment of his slave. Pozzo sarcastically offers Vladimir a handkerchief to wipe away Lucky's tears. As Vladimir approaches the slave, Lucky kicks him.

Pozzo thanks the men for their company by offering them some amusement from Lucky. At first, Lucky speaks about theology but then he starts rambling nonsensically. Pozzo pulls off Lucky's hat, which stops him talking. Pozzo and Lucky leave. Estragon and Vladimir ask each other if they have met Pozzo before.

A boy appears. He claims to be Godot's messenger. He tells the men that Godot can't make it, but he will probably meet them the next day. Vladimir asks if he came the day before implying that the men have been waiting for an indefinite length of time and will continue to do so. As the boy leaves, the moon comes out. The men decide to look for shelter, yet remain standing still.

The next day, Estragon claims he was beaten the night before. Vladimir points out that the tree had no leaves the day before but now it does. Estragon doesn't remember the previous day, but Vladimir points out Estragon's bruise where Lucky kicked him.

They notice that Lucky's hat is still on the ground. They take their hats off and try it on. This turns into a comical hat-swapping scene.

Out of boredom, they sing, eat, exercise, and imitate Pozzo and Lucky.

Pozzo and Lucky re-enter. Lucky is still on a rope, but, this time, the rope is much shorter and Lucky is guiding Pozzo carefully. Pozzo trips over Lucky and they fall on the ground. Because Lucky kicked Estragon, they plan to have a bit of fun with the pair. However, they learn that Pozzo is now blind and Lucky is mute. What is more bizarre is that Pozzo has no recollection of meeting Vladimir and Estragon and he says he will not remember them tomorrow. Pozzo's arrogance and pomposity are gone and he now seems humble and terrified. Pozzo and Lucky exit as Estragon falls asleep.

A messenger boy appears. He seems to be the same boy but Vladimir believes it is the brother of the boy that they saw the day before. Vladimir assumes the boy will give the same message as before and he is correct. Out of frustration, Vladimir chases the boy away. As Estragon awakens, the pair decides to hang themselves. However, Estragon's belt isn't strong enough to support their weight.

They decide to bring a rope the next day so they can hang themselves if Godot doesn't come. They agree that they should leave yet remain standing still.

89.
Lord of the Flies
by William Golding
1954

A group of kids are stranded on an island and attempt to form a society, but they inevitably turn on one another.

A plane full of kids crashes on an uninhabited island after a wartime evacuation. The boys are between the ages of 6-12. One boy, Ralph finds a shell called a conch, which he blows like a horn to locate survivors. Because of his initiative, he is quickly elected as the leader. A small group of boys led by a bully called Jack don't think Ralph deserves to be leader.

Ralph designates some boys to create smoke signals so they can be rescued. At their meetings, it is decided that whoever holds the conch is allowed to speak.

Jack turns his group into hunters. Ralph, Jack, and a boy called Simon form a trinity of leadership. They are the only people who seem to do practical work. The rest of the boys are too young and immature to act practically. All they want to do is play. Ralph's best friend, Piggy is bullied by all of the other boys for his large size and glasses. Simon supervises the building of shelters and tries to make sure the boys are treating each other equally. At first, there is relative peace, but things start to change for the worse. The kids become paranoid once there is talk of a beast on the island. Ralph tells the boys that there is no such monster.

One day, Jack sees a pig and calls the other boys into helping him hunt it. While they successfully catch the pig, a ship sails near the island. It sails on because there was no signal to get its attention. Ralph says it's Jack's fault they weren't rescued.

One night, a battle in the sky occurs. A parachuted man falls onto the island. The body is of a dead pilot who ejected from his plane and got entangled in a tree.

A pair of twins called Sam and Eric see the pilot's body. His parachute makes him look bigger than he is, so the twins think he is the beast. All of the boys are warned that the beast has returned. Jack leads the boys to a mountain of stones called Castle Rock where he claims the beast lives. Ralph insists that there is no such creature. Jack says that Ralph is not strong enough to lead and leaves to form his own group. That night, many of Ralph's group leave to join Jack. Eventually, Ralph, Piggy, and Simon join him too.

Jack's tribe turns animalistic and the boys cover themselves with war paint and perform sacrificial rituals.

Simon wanders off and finds a severed pig's head, which was left as an offering to the beast. Simon has an epileptic fit and imagines the pig is infested with flies and it is talking to him. The pig's head tells Simon that the beast only exists within the boys themselves.

Simon then finds the dead pilot and realizes that there is no beast. He runs to tell the group who are in the middle of a ritual dance. In a frenzy, they mistake Simon as the beast and kill him. Ralph, Piggy, Sam, and Eric feel like they are being corrupted by Jack's ways.

Later, Jack's group steals Piggy's glasses so they can use the lenses to make a fire. Jack's tribe is now based on Castle Rock. Ralph goes there to confront Jack about the theft of Piggy's glasses. One of Jack's boys, Roger drops a rock onto Piggy, killing him.

Ralph runs away, but Jack forces Sam and Eric to join him. The next day, Jack orders his tribe to hunt and kill Ralph. Jack burns the forest to flush Ralph out. As Ralph runs away, he stumbles upon a naval officer who came to inspect the fire. Ralph starts crying and all of the other boys start doing the same.

90.
Atlas Shrugged
by Ayn Rand
1957

A railroad executive and a mogul form an alliance against the increasingly corrupt government.

Dagny Taggart is the Vice President of a railroad company in Colorado. Her brother, Jim is the president of the company. Colorado is the last booming industrial area in the country.

Dagny's first love, Francisco d'Anconia was a successful industrialist that builds rail lines but he has been making bad decisions recently, which will destroy the business. To counter this, Dagny's brother, Jim uses his political influence to annihilate Dagny's competition in Colorado. Dagny uses a new alloy made by Hank Rearden. Hank is a self-made steel businessman that has made Rearden Metal; the most reliable metal worldwide. It causes his competitors to publicly denounce Rearden Metal, which crashes Dagny's business.

Hank and Dagny begin a relationship and join forces in their work. They learn that among the ruins of an abandoned factory, there is an incomplete motor that can convert electricity to kinetic energy. The pair seek out the inventor of this device.

The most successful business leaders suddenly go missing, leaving their companies bankrupt. Dagny believes there is a Destroyer taking out these men. The men's absences cause the economy to collapse, forcing the government to have more control over businesses.

Francisco visits Rearden and asks him why he formed a new business considering the amount of pressure he is under. A fire suddenly breaks out in the mills and Hank desperately tries to put it out. Only then does Francisco see that Hank truly cares about the mills.

An economic dictator called Wesley Mouch befriends Hank because he needs his co-operation to forge new socialist laws. This will help Dagny's brother, Jim out whose business is failing after Colorado's collapse, but he knows it will devastate his sister's and Hank's company. Jim pleads with Hank's wife, Lillian who despises her husband. She divulges the fact that Hank and Dagny are having an affair. Hank finds the new laws restrictive, but he has to sign them, or his affair will become public knowledge, which would ruin Dagny's name.

Dagny finds the new laws too repressive and leaves her company. She receives a letter from the scientist she hired to fix the motor. She tracks him down, believing that he will be the next victim of the Destroyer. She follows him in an airplane, but it crashes. When she wakes up, she finds herself in a remote valley surrounded by the missing business leaders. They are all on strike. She meets John Galt; the man who orchestrated the men's disappearance and the creator of the motor. She falls in love with him.

When she returns to work, she learns that the government has taken control over the railroad industry. The government force Dagny to publicly announce her support for the new law or they will reveal her private relationship with Hank. On the air, Dagny admits she is having an affair and then warns the country about the corruption of the government. The country tears itself apart, affecting crops, transport, and jobs. The government stages a riot at Rearden's mill, but Hank and Francisco join together and form a strike. John Galt takes over the airwaves and announces details to the public about his strike. Galt is captured and tortured by government officials, but Dagny rescues him.

They return to the valley where Dagny joins the strike. Soon after, the country completely collapses without its workers. With the government destroyed, the strikers prepare on their return to reform the country.

91.
Things Fall Apart
by Chinua Achebe
1958

An African tribal leader believes he is unconquerable, but a series of tragic events cause him to have an incontrovertible fall from grace.

This novel takes place in the 1890s in Nigeria before it was colonized. Our main character is Okonkwo; a wrestling champion of the village of Umuofia. He is the leader of his tribe and is respected by all surrounding tribes. He has three wives, several children, and is friends with everyone in the village.

Okonkwo wants to be rich and successful to disassociate himself from his deceased father, Unoka who was known as an effeminate, penniless coward. Okonkwo believes that there is nothing worse than being a loser and coward like his father.

The elders choose Okonkwo to protect a child called Ikemefuna. Ikemefuna was brought to Umuofia as a peace settlement after the child's father killed a woman from that village. Okonkwo takes the boy in and raises him for three years and sees him as his own son.

The Oracle of Umuofia decides that the child must die to pay for his father's transgressions. An old man called Ezeudu warns Okonkwo not to agree to this. But Okonkwo can't show weakness because he saw his worthless father as weak. So, Okonkwo decides that he will kill the child himself.

After the boy's death, Okonkwo feels guilty, which is one of the first times he has ever embraced an emotion apart from anger or pride.

Ezeudu dies shortly after. At his funeral, Okonkwo seems to be cursed. During a gun salute, Okonkwo's gun misfires and shoots Ezeudu's son dead. Okonkwo and his family are banished for seven years. An accidental murder is known as an "ocho" (female kill.) This comes from the idea that women were so weak, they couldn't kill a man on purpose, only by accident. This connotation plagues Okonkwo's ego because he despises the idea of femininity.

While Okonkwo lives in Mbanta, he learns that white men are introducing a religion called Christianity to his old village. Over time, white people seem to control more and more of Okonkwo's former land. One of the missionaries talks to Okonkwo's son, Nwoye, who seems intrigued. Okonkwo pins his son down and threatens him. Nwoye leaves to become a missionary, never to be seen again. Okonkwo realizes that he is losing everything precious to him.

As Okonkwo returns to Umuofia after his exile has ended, he can see that his village has been completely taken over by the white government. Okonkwo and his former followers attempt to reclaim their home by burning a church. The leader of the white government takes them prisoner and holds them for ransom. The prisoners are mocked and tortured.

When Okonkwo is freed, the Umuofians decide to stand up to their oppressors. The government sends a messenger to resolve the matter peacefully but Okonkwo kills him. Okonkwo realizes his people cannot back him now that he has murdered a man. Only then does Okonkwo realize that his battle cannot be won.

When the leader of the government comes to Okonkwo's house to take him to court, he sees that Okonkwo has hanged himself. According to Umuofian beliefs, suicide is the ultimate form of cowardice. Okonkwo will forever be immortalized as a coward.

92.
To Kill a Mockingbird
by Harper Lee
1960

A respected lawyer defends an innocent black man in court from a racist community.

This story takes place during the Great Depression. Atticus Finch is a lawyer who lives in Maycomb, Alabama. He has a daughter called Scout and a son called Jem. They are scared of their neighbor; a mysterious person whom the people of Maycomb refuse to discuss. Although the neighbor is called Arthur, people call him Boo as they imagine him a ghost. They make up stories about Boo like that he eats rats and will kill any child he sees.

One summer, Atticus teaches his children how to shoot with an air rifle. He says that they cannot shoot mockingbirds because these creatures don't kill anything nor do they damage plants or crops. They do no wrong and shouldn't be harmed.

Judge Taylor appoints Atticus to defend a black man called Tom Robinson who is a suspected attacker of a young white woman called Mayella Ewell. Despite disapproval from the town, Atticus takes the case. Other children taunt Atticus' children for loving black people. Atticus meets a group of men who want to hang Tom.

Atticus doesn't want his children to see how horrible and narrow-minded people can be and asks them not to attend the trial. They sneak in but there are no seats left so they watch their father in the trial from the colored balcony.

In the trial, Atticus accuses Mayella and her husband, Bob, (who's known as the town drunk) of lying. It seems that Mayella seduced Tom. Bob discovered her infidelity and it was he that attacked her, not Tom. Tom can't actually physically beat Mayella because his left hand is disabled and her bruises are on the right side.

In spite of this open-and-shut case, the racist jury convicts Tom. On his way to prison, Tom attempts to escape and is shot and killed.

Although Bob won the case, he was humiliated in front of the town. He confronts Atticus and vows revenge on him. Bob spits in his face and storms off.

That Halloween, Bob attacks Jem and Scout with a switchblade. Jem has his arm broken in the attack, but a mysterious man appears to protect Jem. This man is the mysterious Boo! He stabs Bob with a kitchen knife.

The sheriff arrives and learns that Bob has died during the attack. Atticus is worried that his son will be convicted but the sheriff's official report is that Bob accidentally fell on his own knife.

They think it's best if people know Boo killed Bob; not because he would be punished but because he would be rewarded since the town hated Bob. On reflection, the sheriff and Atticus realize that this is a bad idea. The town would give Boo support, which would devastate him because he has been a recluse for years and he will not be able to process so much attention.

Atticus worries that his children will not respect him if they know that he lied about Boo being responsible for Bob's death. Scout says she understands because she doesn't want to do anything that would upset Boo. She believes that to jeopardize Boo's life would be like killing a mockingbird.

93.
Catch-22
by Joseph Heller
1961

A war captain attempts to fake insanity during World War II so he doesn't have to fly missions.

The story takes place during World War II in an Air Force squadron by the Italian coast. The novel revolves around John Yossarian; a 28-year-old captain who is frustrated that his superior officers, Colonel Catchkart and Colonel Korn seem to be thrusting him and the other pilots into suicide missions.

The pilots must fly a set number of missions before they are allowed to return home. However, any time a pilot is about to reach the goal, the colonels sneakily raise the mission quota.

Yossarian seems to be the only person in his squadron who's aware of the army's manipulation and the rest of the men view him as being paranoid.

He keeps thinking of a soldier he knew called Snowden, who died in his arms in spite of Yossarian's best efforts to save him.

This incident is what destroyed any passion Yossarian may have had for war. He now sees war as a sham rather than a heroic deed.

Yossarian sees friends die, his squadron gets bombed (by its own officer) and generals lead their men into death traps in order to improve their reputations.

Yossarian learns that if a pilot is insane, he will be discharged. He fakes insanity and many illnesses to avoid the war but to no avail. Faking insanity can't work because of a law known as Catch-22. It states that if a person is able to recognize he is insane, he must be sane because a truly insane person would believe he is sane.

Yossarian has a friend called Nately who assumed that the war was coming to an end. He enlisted under the impression that he wouldn't have to fight and would be admired for his bravery for the rest of his life.

Nately falls in love with a Roman prostitute who is only refered to as "Nately's Whore." At first, she is not interested but over time, she falls in love with him. Tragically, he gets killed in a mission soon after.

Yossarian is the one to notify her of Nately's demise. She blames Yossarian and tries to stab him every time she sees him.

Over time, Yossarian becomes depressed over Nately's death. He feels responsible for watching another friend die. He adamantly refuses to fly any more missions. As he wanders through Rome, he sees the worst side of humanity on the streets – disease, famine, and murder.

He is eventually arrested for not having a pass. Colonel Catchcart and Colonel Korn approach him and say Yossarian can avoid jail if he states that he supports their policy (which is to fly 80 missions.) He's tempted to take their offer, but he refuses on the grounds that he would be leading innocent men to their deaths.

Instead, he decides to flee to neutral Sweden and try to regain control of his disillusioned life.

94.
Dune
by Frank Herbert
1965

The son of a Duke leads desert warriors against the galactic empire.

21,000 years into the future, mankind inhabits several planets ruled by Emperor Shaddam. In spite of vast technological leaps over the millenia, AI and computers are illegal. With no access to most technology, some of humanity have evolved with psychic powers. These people are called Mentats and they can do analytical calculations like a computer.

A matriarch called Bene Gesserit intends to lead humanity by controlled breeding. To help maintain a high standard of breeding, she relies on a spice called "mélange" which can extend a person's lifespan and makes one capable of seeing into the future for a brief time. Melange only exists on a desert planet called Arrakis, which is populated by people called Fremen who believe a messiah will save them one day.

Emperor Shaddam grants Duke Leto of House Atreides control of the mélange mine on Arrakis. Leto believes it's a trap but he goes along with it.

Gesserit was ordered to use the breeding program to make sure Leto and his partner, Jessica, only bred daughters. Nevertheless, Jessica gives birth to a baby boy called Paul. Even though Jessica was programmed to have a girl, she overrode it with the power of love. Realising that this shows the unreliability of the breeding programme, Gesserit's reputation is in jeopardy.

The Atreides land on Arrakis and Leto befriends the Fremen. As presumed, Shaddam set a trap for Leto as the emperor's warriors capture him. Jessica is pregnant so Paul takes her away from any potential harm. Leto tragically dies in captivity. Paul and Jessica ally with the Fremen. The Fremen teach Paul how to fight and Jessica is given the Water of Life; a liquid that will grant her unborn daughter, Alia, the same power as Gesserit. Paul falls for a girl called Chani and they have a son.

Four years later, Paul, Jessica, and Alia's powers grow after years of exposure to mélange. Paul's ability to see into the future becomes so advanced, the Fremen believe he is the messiah and gives himself the Fremen name, Muad'Dib.

Shaddam becomes concerned about the "Muad'Dib" ruining his plans. A rival of the Atreides, Baron Harkonnen has a nephew called Glossu who rules Arrakis. He intends to replace Glossu with his heir, Feyd. Feyd is more reasonable than Glossu so the Baron assumes the people of Arrakis will listen to him.

Doubting the strength of his visions, Paul drinks the Water of Life. After a few weeks, he becomes accustomed to his new powers. He is now able to see into the past, the present, and into future of all men and women. He can see that the Emperor has prepared an armada to fight against the planet. The invasion causes the capture of Alia and the death of his son. Alia is brought to the planet's capital, Arrakeen.

But the Fremens attack the capital by riding huge sandworms. This distraction gives Alia a chance to kill Baron Harkonnen. Paul confronts the Emperor and threatens to use his powers to destroy all mélange, therefore crippling the empire. The Emperor makes peace by offering his daughter to Paul. Paul takes the throne and control over Arrakis. He uses the mélange to bring peace to the galaxy but sees attacks in his visions for the future and worries that he won't be able to stop them.

95.
Slaughterhouse Five
by Kurt Vonnegut
1969

An American soldier is traumatised after World War II and tries to ingratiate himself back into society.

Billy Pilgrim is an American soldier who doesn't want to fight in a war. During the Battle of the Bulge in 1944, the Germans capture him among other soldiers. By the time he is caught, Billy is on the verge of death. He is captured with Roland; a bully who mocks Billy for not wanting to go to war. Roland has all of his possessions confiscated, including his boots and is forced to wear wooden clogs. Eventually, Roland dies from gangrene caused by the clogs. Before he dies, Roland tells another prisoner called Paul Lazarro that Billy is responsible. Lazzaro vows to kill Billy.

Billy is so traumatized that he starts to relive his past memories. Billy misinterprets this as travelling through time.

A year later, the prisoners are transported to Dresden in Germany. Billy and the other prisoners are put into a former slaughterhouse. They call this building Schlachthof-funt, which translates into "Slaughterhouse Five."

When bombs go off outside, the prisoners and Germans of Slaughterhouse Five hide in the cellar. Because of the resilience of the cellar, they are among the only survivors of the Dresden attacks. When World War II ends, Billy is transported back to America where he receives an honorable discharge from service.

Although the war is over, Billy has to be institutionalized because he is suffering from post traumatic stress disorder. He meets a man called Eliot Rosewater in the institution who introduces him to some science fiction books by Kilgore Trout.

Billy eventually gets released, marries an unattractive and obese woman called Valencia Merble and becomes an optometrist. Billy and Valencia have two children, Robert and Barbara.

Barbara grows up and gets engaged and on her wedding night, Billy gets abducted by toilet-plunger shaped aliens and he is taken billions of miles away to a planet called Tralfamadore.Billy meets a beautiful woman called Montana Wildhack who has also been abducted. They fall in love and have a child. Billy is eventually sent back to Earth.

In 1968, Billy and a copilot are the only survivors of a plane crash. While Billy is recovering in hospital, Valencia dies from carbon monoxide poisoning while driving to see her husband.

In Billy's hospital room, there is a history professor called Bertram Rumfoord. Billy talks about the Dresden bombing and Bertram says it was a necessary attack.

Billy's daughter takes him home. He leaves the house without telling anybody and checks into a hotel in New York. He wanders around Times Square and visits a bookstore. In the store, he sees some Kilgore Trout books and reads through them.

That night, he goes on a radio show and talks about his time-travelling adventures and his journey to an alien planet until the studio kick him out.

He goes back to his hotel and time-travels back to 1945 Dresden where the story concludes.

96.
Watership Down
by Richard Adams
1972

A colony of rabbits try to survive after leaving their warren.

Fiver is the runt of a colony of rabbits. He lives in a warren in Sandleford. He has a vision that his home will be annihilated. Fiver alerts his chief that they must evacuate the warren, but he doesn't listen. Fiver and his brother, Hazel, and several other rabbits leave of their own accord.

Hazel was never an important rabbit in the warren, but he finds himself the leader of the group. Their party includes the bodyguards of the warren, Bigwig and Silver. Bodyguards are known as Owlsa.

They eventually meet another rabbit called Cowslip who encourages the rabbits to join his warren.

Bigwig is nearly killed in a snare designed to trap rabbits. Cowslip panics because he says he desperately needs an Owlsa like Bigwig. The other rabbits realize that Cowslip only wanted them to increase his own colony's numbers to boost the chances of his warren's survival. Fiver's group continues to look for a new home.

The rabbits eventually find a place called Watership Down, which looks like a perfectly suitable place to form a warren.

Over time, rabbits from the original warren start to appear. Two rabbits called Holly and Bluebell come from the Sandleford Warren and inform Fiver that he was right and humans have destroyed their warren.

Watership Down seems like an ideal home but Hazel knows they will have problems in the future because there are no does (female rabbits,) only bucks (male rabbits.) With the help of a black-headed gull called Kehaar, they find a warren called Efrafa, which is full of does.

Hazel sends a small group to Efrafa to explain their predicament. In the mean time, Hazel and another rabbit called Pipkin check out a nearby farm called Nuthanger Farm, which is guarded by a watchdog. Hazel raids the farm the following day and rescues three rabbits.

Upon their return, Hazel finds that the rabbits that he despatched to Efrafa have returned but they are injured. It turns out that a tyrant rabbit called General Woundwort controls Efrafa with an iron fist. One doe of Efrafa called Hyzenthlay told the recruiting rabbits that she will encourage many of her colony to leave Efrafa and join Watership Down. Hazel and Bigwig help form a plan to allow the Efrafans to join their warren.

Not long after, the Owsla of Efrafa arrive in Watership Down. They are led by Woundwort who intends to attack the warren. Hazel has a plan to defeat Woundwort. Hazel and Bigwig head back to the Nuthanger Farm. Hazel gnaws at the watchdog's rope until it is released. Bigwig runs and the dog gives chase.

The dog chases Bigwig all the way back to Watership Down. In spite of the dog's ferocity, Woundwort engages it in combat. The outcome of the fight is ambiguous. The dog is badly injured but Woundwort's body is missing.

Some time passes and Hazel is greeted by the deity of the rabbits, El-ahrairah. He encourages Hazel to join him as one of his own Owsla. Hazel leaves his friends, his home (and his physical body) to join El-ahrairah.

97.
The Stand
by Stephen King
1978

A plague kills most of the world's population leading the forces of good and evil to prepare their armies for the final battle.

A weaponized strain of flu is leaked from an American Army base and one of the soldiers becomes exposed. He spreads the virus to his family and within less than a month, it has become an apocalyptic pandemic, killing off over 99% of the world's population.

Very few people seem to be immune to the virus. The survivors try to rebuild society. However, they start to experience hallucinations of a 108-year-old woman called Mother Abagail from Nebraska. She is seen as the embodiment of good and the survivors track her down, believing that she will be their savior. In these visions, she tells the survivors to form a society in Colorado called the Free Zone. The survivors make their way to Abagail's home and she prepares to reform society.

However, survivors that harbor evil experience an alternative hallucination. They have dreams of a man from Las Vegas called Randall Flagg who embodies pure evil and promises to save the strong and kill the weak.

Under Flagg's supervision, they are able to reform society, restore power and build a weapons programme. Flagg intends to obtain all of America's remaining weapons so he can rule the world.

Abagail leaves her home to find spiritual peace in the wilderness. In her absence, two of the survivors called Harold and Nadine who are staying with Abagail have visions of Flagg. He tempts them with ultimate power if they join his cause. Flagg's manipulation works and Nadine and Harold turn on the rest of the Free Zone survivors. They use a bomb to try and exterminate the committee. Luckily, no one is killed.

However, they learn that Abagail is dying. Just before she dies, Abagail sends four survivors – Glen, Stu, Ralph, and Larry to Las Vegas to try and come to a peaceful understanding with Flagg.

Stu breaks his leg on the way. He demands that the others go on without him believing that God has a plan for everyone. As the other three arrive in Las Vegas, Flagg's army captures them. Flagg orders Glen to kneel before him. Glen refuses and is slaughtered.

Flagg gathers his entire army to witness the execution of Ralph and Larry. As they are about to be killed, one of Flagg's followers known as the Trashcan Man appears with a stolen nuclear warhead.

Suddenly, an enormous glowing hand known as The Hand of God appears and detonates the nuke, killing everyone in Las Vegas, including Ralph and Larry.

Back in Colorado, Stu's love interest, Frances is about to have a baby. No known babies have been born since the pandemic so they worry that the child may not have immunity to the superflu.

The baby is born and is named Peter. He survives the flu, proving that humanity will prevail. Stu returns after being rescued by another Free Zone survivor.

The book ends with Flagg waking up on a beach in the South Pacific. He has no memory of who he is. The island's inhabitants see Flagg as a deity.

98.
Beloved
by Toni Morrison
1987

A former slave is permanently haunted by her dark past when a mysterious woman appears at her doorstep.

This story is about Sethe and her daughter, Denver escaping from enslavement. Denver is reclusive and has not ventured outside for years. They live in a house in Cincinnati that was owned by Sethe's mother-in-law, Baby Suggs, who is now deceased. Their home is apparently haunted by a ghost.

Paul D arrives at Sethe's house. Paul D was enslaved at the same plantation as Baby Suggs and Sethe.

Paul D begins a relationship with Sethe. He exorcises the house of the ghost and reminds them that they can't live in fear nor can they hide from the past. He makes Denver go outside for the first time in years. They go for a walk and as they return to their house, they see a woman who calls herself Beloved. Paul D is suspicious of her but Sethe seems surprisingly inviting to the stranger and accepts her into the house.

Paul D decides to sleep in the shed after he feels a dark presence in the house. Beloved confronts him in the shed, and they sleep together. Paul D feels guilty and tries to tell Sethe, but he chickens out and instead tells her he wants to start a family with her. Sethe is overjoyed. Paul D tells his friends at work that he is going to marry Sethe but they warn him to stay away from her.

Paul D asks Sethe about what happened to her after she escaped from her slave master. She has no choice but to tell him the truth. When she escaped from her slave farm, Sweet Home, she ran to Baby Suggs' house.

When her slave owner came to the county to reobtain his "property," Sethe panicked and took her children to the tool shed and tried to kill them. She only succeeded in killing her two-year-old daughter by running a saw along her neck. Sethe claims that she was "trying to put my babies where they would be safe." Her daughter's tombstone only said one word, "Beloved." Paul D can't accept this and he leaves.

Sethe believes the woman that is staying in the house is the reincarnation of her murdered daughter. In a desperate attempt to undo her horrid past, she gives Beloved everything she could desire. Beloved becomes spoilt and prone to tantrums when she doesn't get what she wants. Sethe neglects herself and withers away as Beloved becomes bigger and bigger.

Now that Denver has overcome her isolation and can venture outside, she asks the community to help her mother. Some women show up at Sethe's house to tell her that they forgive her for murdering Beloved. They understand that she is not evil, and she did what she believed was right. They hope to exorcise Beloved from the community.

A white friend of Baby Sugg's comes to offer Denver a job. Sethe sees him and becomes terrified because he is white. Afraid that he will take her children away, Sethe stabs him to death with an ice pick.

Beloved disappears. Denver becomes a part of the working community. Paul D returns to Sethe to tell her he still loves her.

99.
The Remains of the Day
by Kazuo Ishiguro
1989

A butler dedicates his life to his service before he realizes how misguided his loyalty is.

The novel begins in 1956. An English butler called Stevens works in Darlington Hall for a rich American called Mr. Farraday. Stevens buttled for 34 years for the now-deceased Lord Darlington before Farraday became the current owner of the estate. Stevens finds Farraday to be a nice man but doesn't go out of his way to socialize with him. Stevens is a very serious man and doesn't know how to banter like his employer.

Farraday is about to take a trip to America and advises Stevens to take a well-earned week off. Stevens dismisses the idea at first. However, he receives a letter from a woman he's loved for years called Miss Kenton. She was the housekeeper for Darlington 20 years ago. Stevens believes that the letter implies that she is unhappy with her husband and she wishes to return to work as housekeeper in Darlington Hall. Stevens takes a six-day trip to visit Miss Kenton.

Stevens begins his journey and reflects on his past during and after World War II. He reminisces about his father, who was also a butler. He began work at Darlington Hall in his 70s and he suffered arthritis, so he struggled with his job. Stevens tried to share the workload with his father. This was awkward as they spoke less and less as the years went by.

One night, as the staff were entertaining a party, Miss Kenton informs Stevens that his father is ill. Stevens returns to his duties, but Darlington can see he is getting emotional. To preserve his dignity, he says his emotion is simply from a tiring day.

Miss Kenton comes up to Stevens shortly after to tell him that his father has just died. Stevens continues with his duties and he is proud of his professionalism as a butler. For Stevens, preserving his professional dignity is his highest priority. Even when Miss Kenton tries to speak to him as a friend rather than as colleagues, Stevens remains professional and points out that her manner is inappropriate.

Stevens remembers when Miss Kenton's only relative died. Miss Kenton was extremely distressed but because of Stevens's manner, he didn't know how to speak to her except in a purely professional manner. Stevens and Miss Kenton were in love but never acted on it nor did they confess their love to each other. On reflection, Stevens now worries that if he was there for Miss Kenton when her relative died, maybe things would've turned out differently between them.

Stevens has entertained many parties over the years. Over time, the parties died down because Lord Darlington supported the Nazi regime before their true intentions became clear. He even invited Nazis and British heads of state to his estate to come to a peaceful resolution. Stevens firmly believes that Darlington was a good man at heart who misread the Nazis' evil schemes.

Stevens eventually arrives at Miss Kenton's home. She admits to Stevens that her life would have turned out much better if she married him instead of her husband, Mr. Benn. But Kenton said she got over it because she can't dwell on a past that she can't change. Stevens agrees and tries to move on.

Stevens returns to Darlington Hall alone. His only objective now is to perfect "bantering" for the sake of Mr. Farraday.

100.
The Kite Runner
by Khaled Hosseini
2003

Amir returns to Afghanistan to help his friend's troubled son.

The story begins in 1974. Amir and Hassan are two Afghan kids who often fly kites together in Kabul. Hassan's father, Ali is the servant of Amir's father, Baba. Hassan is an excellent kite runner and can do all sorts of tricks. Baba loves both children but is very harsh on Amir, believing him to be weak and cowardly. Amir sees Baba's friend, Rahim as a father. Rahim encourages Amir's passion for writing.

A blond, white bully called Assef taunts Amir for being friends with Hassan, whom he believes is inferior because he has a cleft lip. Assef is about to beat Amir with brass knuckles but Hassan threatens to shoot his eye out with a slingshot. Assef backs off.

Amir wins the kite tournament and Baba is very proud of him. Hassan runs to collect his kite but is confronted by Assef in an alleyway. Assef beats him and abuses him. Amir witnesses the act but is too scared to intervene. His priority is to bring back his kite to his father to earn the praise that he so desperately craves. Getting emotional over the attack on his friend would make him look weak in his father's eyes. Because of this, Amir avoids Hassan. To avoid feeling guilty, Amir plants valuables underneath Hassan's mattress. When Baba discovers them and confronts Hassan, Hassan knows that he is no longer wanted and falsely admits that he stole them. Hassan and his father leave.

Five years later, militia from the Soviet Union enter Afghanistan. Amir and Baba escape to Pakistan and then to California. They settle in a grungy apartment.

Amir graduates from high school and goes to college where he hopes he will continue his passion for writing. Amir and Baba make extra money selling used goods at a flea market where they meet another refugee called Soraya and her family. Baba learns he is dying of cancer and he asks Soraya's father if he will allow his daughter to marry Amir. The father agrees and the two get married. Baba dies soon after.

After Amir and Soraya move in together, they learn that they can't have children. Amir begins his writing career.

15 years after they got married, Amir gets a phonecall from a terminally ill Rahim who tells him to return home. When Amir returns to Afghanistan, Rahim informs him that Ali was killed by a land mine. Hassan and his wife were killed after Hassan stopped the Taliban from confiscating Amir's old house. Rahim also tells Amir that Ali was sterile, so Hassan was not his son. Hassan was Baba's son and Amir's half-brother. Finally, Rahim tells Amir that Hassan's son, Sohrab is currently in an orphanage in Kabul and he wants Amir to find him.

Amir and a war veteran called Farid seek out Sohrab. They discover that a Taliban officer comes to the orphanage often and pays the management so he can take one of the girls. Recently though, he took one of the boys – Sohrab. With Farid's aid, they locate the officer at his home.

What they don't realize is that the officer is actually Assef. Assef has been abusing Sohrab and is forcing him to dance in women's clothing. Assef says he will give up Sohrab if he can beat up Amir. As Assef beats Amir, Sohrab pulls out a slingshot and shoots out Assef's left eye. Amir is taken to America and he is legally adopted. Sohrab doesn't socialize with Amir or Soraya at first. But when they show him a kite trick, Sohrab offers a lopsided smile, insinuating that he will embrace them eventually.

Printed in Great Britain
by Amazon